AF882425

SOTHIS PRESS

Sothis Press aims to completely reimagine the public domain book with an emphasis on universal access to captivatingly designed print editions. We believe that technology will enable every single book ever published to be perpetually accessible in beautiful print form. Sothis is beauty in ubiquity.

www.sothis.press
1 Waterhouse Square, London, EC1N 2ST

The Seisin of the Freehold

Being Twelve Lectures Delivered in
Gray's Inn Hall in the Months
of January and February, 1876

Joshua Williams

SOTHIS PRESS

ISBN 978-1-0368-0086-4

The Seisin of the Freehold
is in the public domain.

This edition is published by

The company
is registered in England and Wales.
The Company Number is 14900389.

THE

SEISIN OF THE FREEHOLD,

BEING

Twelve Lectures

DELIVERED IN GRAY'S INN HALL

IN THE MONTHS OF

JANUARY AND FEBRUARY, 1876.

BY

JOSHUA WILLIAMS, Esq.,

OF LINCOLN'S INN, ONE OF HER MAJESTY'S COUNSEL,

PROFESSOR OF THE LAW OF REAL AND PERSONAL PROPERTY TO THE COUNCIL OF LEGAL EDUCATION.

LONDON:

H. SWEET, 3, CHANCERY LANE,

Law Publisher;

C. F. MAXWELL, MELBOURNE.

1878.

LONDON:

PRINTED BY C. F. ROWORTH, BREAM'S BUILDINGS, CHANCERY LANE.

PREFACE.

THESE Lectures are printed nearly verbatim as they were delivered. The Author, however, has not scrupled to add and alter in a few places where amendment seemed desirable. The principal additions are the remarks on quasi estates tail in leaseholds and copyholds for lives at the end of Lectures X. and XI. A few authorities are occasionally given in the notes. The Author has added in Appendix (A.) a few remarks on heriots, and in Appendix (B.) he has given the text of the Act 40 & 41 Vict. c. 33, to amend the law as to contingent remainders, with a few remarks thereon. He has been assisted in preparing these Lectures for the press by his son Mr. T. CYPRIAN WILLIAMS, of Lincoln's Inn, barrister-at-law, to whom also he is indebted for the Index.

3, STONE BUILDINGS, LINCOLN'S INN,
4th February, 1878.

TABLE OF CONTENTS.

LECTURE IV.

LECTURE V.

LECTURE VI.

Lecture VII.

Lecture VIII.

LECTURE IX.

LECTURE X.

LECTURE XI.

LECTURE XII.

INDEX TO CASES CITED.

ERRATA.

Page 75, line 14 from bottom, *for* "of the case" *read* "in the case."
Page 89, line 18 from bottom, *for* "The ninth canon" *read* "The seventh canon," and in marginal note, *for* "9th rule" *read* "7th rule."
Page 109, marginal note, *for* "No claim after fines" *read* "Non-claim after fines."

SEISIN OF THE FREEHOLD.

LECTURE I.

The subject of the present course of Lectures is the *Seisin of the Freehold* as it affects—

1st. Tenure;
2nd. Descent;
3rd. Conveyance;
4th. Settlement.

I have chosen this subject because it appears to me to be a good illustration of the growth of our English laws of real property. Some of the most remarkable of these laws, viewed by themselves, apart from their history, and judged only by the benefits which now result from them, appear to me to be absolutely worthless. Others are worse than worthless; they are absurd and injurious; but how they came where they are is not unaccountable. The apology, and that I fear a poor one, for their presence is, that at one time they were integral parts of a system, long since passed away, but which, while it existed, was not irrational, nor unsuited to the times in which it flourished. In fact it is impossible to understand our English laws of real property without some reference to their history. To learn what is now the law, you must necessarily learn a great deal of what once was law, but is now law no longer. It is history which gives coherence to points of law, and enables you to pick up one without dropping another.

In beginning by going back to the early history of our land laws, I think I shall best perform my allotted task; and I shall not, I hope, unduly trench on the province of my learned coadjutor (*a*), to whom the very important subject of legal history has, with not a few others, been assigned.

Definition of seisin of the freehold.

Seisin of the freehold may be defined to be the possession of such an estate in land as was anciently thought worthy to be held by a free man. Such an estate is called in law an estate of freehold. Seisin, in Latin *seisina* or *saisina*, simply means possession. It seems to be derived from the verb *saisiare* or *saisire*, to seize or take possession of. The articles which the barons presented for the acceptance of King John provide (*b*)—"Rex vel ballivus non *saisiet* terram aliquam pro debito dum catalla debitoris sufficiunt." And the Magna Charta of that king accordingly declares (*c*)—"Nec nos nec ballivi nostri *seisiemus* terram aliquam nec redditum pro debito aliquo, quamdiu catalla debitoris sufficiunt ad debitum reddendum." According to Mr. Stubbs, the Regius Professor of Modern History in the University of Oxford (*d*), this word *saisiare* or *saisire* is derived from the old High German word *sazjan*. This derivation of the word *seisin* is certainly suggestive; for, if that of which a man has seisin literally means that which a man has seized, we are landed at once in the times when

"Prevailed the good old plan—
That he is right who has the might,
And he shall keep who can."

In these days of peace and policemen, it is not very easy to realize the lawlessness of the times in which our early legal terms took root. Mr. Watkins, in his Essay on the Law of Descent (*e*), refers to an old case,

(*a*) Sir Edward Creasy.
(*b*) Article 5.
(*c*) Sect. 9.
(*d*) Stubbs's Select Charters, p. 548.
(*e*) Page 53, 4th ed.

in the eighth book of the Assizes and Pleas of the Crown, held before the justices in the time of Edward III. (*f*), in which one entering into a house by the window, when half out and half in, was pulled out by the heels; and in this case the entry was adjudged sufficient to give him seisin of the house. In the Tenures of Littleton, who was a judge in the reign of King Edward IV., and whose name, says Coke, is not the name of the author only, but the law itself, will be found a considerable amount of learning on the question, how a person, whose lands have been wrongfully seized by another, may keep up his legal title to them. The doctrine which he discusses is that of *continual claim*, and it forms the subject of the seventh chapter of Littleton's Third Book. If a man was dis-seised or deprived of his seisin, he might keep up his right to enter the lands of which he was dis-seised, by making continual claim to them. This was done as follows:— "If," says Littleton (*g*), "a man hath title to enter into any lands or tenements, if he dares not enter into the same lands or tenements, nor into any parcel thereof, for doubt of beating, or for doubt of maiming, or for doubt of death, if he goeth and approach as near to the tenements as he dare for such doubt, and by word claim the lands to be his, presently by such claim *he hath a possession and seisin in the lands*, as well as if he had entered in deed, although he never had possession or seisin of the same lands or tenements before the same claim." To this section Lord Coke adds the following commentary (*h*):—"Here it is to be observed that every doubt or fear is not sufficient, for it must concern the safety of the person of a man, and not his houses or goods; for if he fear the burning of his houses, or the taking away or spoiling of his goods, this is not sufficient; because he

Entry.

Continual claim.

(*f*) Folio 17 b.
(*g*) Sect. 419.
(*h*) Coke upon Littleton, 253 b.

may recover the same, or damages to the value, without any corporal hurt."

Acquisition of right by entry and by continual claim not abolished till 1833.

Entries and claims of this nature were very well suited to rough and early times; but one can hardly imagine such scenes having taken place in the present century. So tardy however is the progress of remedial legislation, that it was not until the year 1833 that the acquisition of right by mere entry and by continual claim was abolished. The act for the limitation of actions and suits relating to real property, and for simplifying the remedies for trying the rights thereto (*i*), provides (*k*) that no person shall be deemed to have been in possession of any land within the meaning of that act, merely by reason of having made an entry thereon; and (*l*) that no continual or other claim upon or near any land shall preserve any right of making an entry or distress, or of bringing an action.

Seisin is possession.

Seisin then, however acquired, is simply possession. The word is now confined to the possession of an estate of freehold. But in early times the word seems to have been not unfrequently used in its simple primary meaning of possession, without any regard to the estate of the possessor. Thus Bracton, who wrote in the reign of Henry III., speaks in one place (*m*) of restoring to a leaseholder for a term of years, the seisin of land from which he had been ejected,—an expression which would now be considered inaccurate, as an estate for a certain term of years is not an estate of freehold, as we shall see bye-and-bye. So Littleton (*n*) speaks of a man holding tenements for a term of years, "by force of which lease the lessee is seised." At the present time, however, the word *seisin* is exclusively applied to

(*i*) Stat. 3 & 4 Will. 4, c. 27.
(*k*) Sect. 10.
(*l*) Sect. 11.
(*m*) Book 4, c. 36.
(*n*) Sect. 567.

the possession of an estate of freehold. And in ancient times the possession of the freehold was the rule; the possession of a leaseholder was looked upon as merely the possession of a bailiff or farmer, and was in fact an exceptional case. If a farmer were ejected, he had, in ancient times, no remedy beyond an action for damages against his landlord, who was bound to warrant him quiet possession. His possession was in truth regarded by the law as the actual possession of his landlord, the freeholder. Thus, suppose a man to have two farms, Whiteacre and Blackacre, of both of which he is the freeholder, and in both of which he has an estate in fee simple in possession. Whiteacre he keeps in his own occupation; Blackacre he lets to a yearly tenant. He then dies intestate. His heir-at-law is not actually seised of Whiteacre, the possession of which became vacant on his ancestor's death, until he enters and takes possession. But of Blackacre he is, in contemplation of law, *actually seised* from the moment of his ancestor's decease, for the possession of a yearly tenant is looked upon as the landlord's own possession. Of Whiteacre he is said to have merely a seisin in law, until actual entry. Of Blackacre he has an actual seisin, or seisin in deed, by reason of the occupation of his yearly tenant, which in law is looked upon as his own.

Actual seisin.

Seisin in law.

Seisin then is not only possession, but it is the possession of an estate of freehold, or such an estate as was anciently considered to be worthy to be held by a free man. The smallest estate of freehold is an estate for the life of the holder, or for the life of another person. A man cannot have an estate for life in possession without having also the seisin of the freehold. Another estate of freehold, of which I hope to say more hereafter, is an estate tail, or an estate limited to a man and the heirs of his body generally; or it may be limited to the heirs male of his body, in which case it can only descend

An estate of freehold.

Estate for life.

Estate tail.

to males descended from males; or to the heirs female of his body, in which case it can only descend to females descended from females. Or an estate tail may be limited specially to a man's heirs by a particular wife, a mode of limitation now obsolete. The tenant of an estate tail in possession has necessarily the seisin of the freehold, in the same manner as a tenant for life. But by far the most important and usual estate of freehold is an estate in fee simple, or an estate given to a man and his heirs. A tenant in fee simple in possession is necessarily seised of the freehold. It is to estates in fee simple that my remarks will at present be confined.

Fee simple.

A man who is seised of land for an estate of fee simple is said to be seised thereof *in his demesne as of fee*. This expression is as old as the times of Glanville, who wrote in the reign of Henry II. He gives (*o*) a form of a writ to be sued out by the son and heir of the deceased owner of an estate in fee in a yard-land (*virgata terræ*), in order to recover possession of it. Twelve free and lawful men of the neighbourhood of the vill or township in which the lands were situate, were to be summoned before the king or his justices upon a certain day, in order to ascertain by oath whether the father of the person suing out the writ was *seised in his demesne as of fee* of the lands in question in that township on the day that he died. The words of the writ are:—"Si T. pater praedicti G. fuit seisitus in dominico suo sicut de feodo suo de unâ virgatâ terræ in illa villa die quâ obiit."

In his demesne as of fee.

The owner of an estate in fee is seised *in dominico suo*, in his demesne; that is, the land is retained by himself under his own dominion, for his own use, and has not been granted out by him to any other freeholder to be holden by such freeholder as his tenant. And he

Demesne.

(*o*) Book 13, c. 3.

As of fee.

is seised in his demesne *sicut de feodo suo*, as of his fee, or as of fee; that is to say, he is seised or possessed of an estate, which he himself feudally holds of another person. Here we have two main principles of law. First, that none but a freeholder can have feudal seisin; and secondly, that every freeholder is himself the tenant of some lord.

Possession is *primâ facie* evidence of seisin in fee.

In former days estates in fee simple largely predominated over estates of a lesser kind. There were not then so many settlements as there are now on persons for life, with remainders over to other persons. And the rule of law still is, and it is a rule of great importance, that the mere *possession of land is primâ facie evidence of a seisin in fee* (*p*). I say *primâ facie* evidence, for the presumption may be rebutted by evidence, showing that the possessor has in fact a less estate (*q*). But, in the absence of any such evidence, the person found in possession will, to the present day, be presumed to be seised in his demesne as of fee.

Estate by wrong an estate in fee.

There is another rule still in existence, founded apparently on the same principles, and that rule is, that *an estate gained by wrong is always an estate in fee simple* (*r*). If a person wrongfully gets possession of the land of another, he becomes wrongfully entitled to an estate in fee simple, and to no less estate in that land; thus, if a squatter wrongfully encloses a bit of waste land, and builds a hut on it and lives there, he acquires an estate in fee simple by his own wrong in the land which he

(*p*) *Jayne* v. *Price*, 5 Taunt. 326; *Doe* d. *Daniel* v. *Coulthred*, 7 Ad. & Ell. 239, per Lord Denman; *Doe* d. *Graham* v. *Penfold*, 8 Car. & Payne, 536, per Patteson, J.

(*q*) *Metters* v. *Brown*, 1 Hurls. & Colt. 686, 692.

(*r*) "Wrong is unlimited and ravens all that can be gotten, and is not governed by terms of the estates, because it is not contained within rules."—Hobart, p. 323; Co. Litt. 180 b, n. (7). See also Co. Litt. 271 a.

has enclosed. He is seised, and the owner of the waste is dis-seised. It is true that until, by length of time, the Statute of Limitations shall have confirmed his title, he may be turned out by legal process. But as long as he remains, he is not a mere tenant at will, nor for years, nor for life, nor in tail; but he has an estate in fee simple. He has seisin of the freehold to him and his heirs. The rightful owner, meantime, has but a right of entry, a right in many respects equivalent to seisin; but he is not actually seised, for if one person is seised, another person cannot be so.

Having thus endeavoured to explain what seisin of the freehold is, I now proceed to the first branch of my subject, namely, this—

Seisin as it affects tenure.

The seisin of the freehold as it affects TENURE.

In order to explain this matter, it will be necessary to go back into the times which preceded the passing of the

Statute of *Quia emptores.*

Statute of *Quia emptores*, which was passed in the eighteenth year of the reign of King Edward I. (*s*). This statute still exercises an important influence on transactions relating to landed property. The reasons for its passing have long ceased to exist; but it still remains upon the Statute Book, and can only be explained by a reference to the circumstances which gave rise to it.

In ancient times, then, the alienation of land took

Subinfeudation.

place almost universally by what is called *subinfeudation*. The owner of the land, that is, the man who, in legal language, was seised of it in his demesne as of fee, if he wished to part with a portion of it, was in the habit of conveying it to his grantee and his heirs, to

(*s*) Chap. 1.

hold of himself and his heirs, at certain rents and services. Numerous examples of these ancient grants are to be found in the Formulare Anglicanum of Mr. Madox. The usual form of grant runs thus:—*Tenendum de me et hæredibus meis sibi et hæredibus suis.*

The effect of such a grant as this was to make the grantee the tenant of the grantor. At the time of the grant, possession was delivered, by what was called *livery of seisin*, and thereafter the grantee became seised of the land in his demesne as of fee, holding feudally to himself and his heirs of the grantor and his heirs. The grantor, therefore, was no longer seised of the land in question; but he was the lord, and, as such lord, he had a right to the rent reserved, and to the services specified in the deed of grant, whatever they might have been. That which the grantor had was called, and is called still, a *seignory or lordship*.

Livery of seisin.

A *seignory*.

Now to the seignory or lordship of land in ancient times there were incident divers benefits, which, though of great advantage to the lord, were very burdensome to the tenant. The first incident was *homage*, which is thus described by Littleton in his Tenures (*t*):—"Homage is the most honourable service and most humble service of reverence that a frank tenant may do to his lord. For when the tenant shall make homage to his lord he shall be ungirt, and his head uncovered, and his lord shall sit, and the tenant shall kneel before him on both his knees, and hold his hands jointly together between the hands of his lord, and shall say this, 'I become your man from this day forward, of life and limb and of earthly worship, and unto you shall be true and faithful and bear to you faith for the tene-

Homage.

(*t*) Sects. 85, 86 and 87.

ments that I claim to hold of you, saving the faith that I owe unto our sovereign lord the king;' and then the lord so sitting shall kiss him." But if an abbot or a prior or other man of religion shall do homage to his lord, he shall not say, "I become your man, &c.," for that he hath professed himself to be only the man of God; but he shall say thus, "I do homage unto you, and to you I shall be true and faithful, and faith to you bear for the tenements which I hold of you, saving the faith which I do owe unto our lord the king." Also if a woman sole shall do homage, she shall not say, "I become your woman," for it is not fitting that a woman should say that she will become a woman to any man but to her husband, when she is married. But she shall say, "I do you homage, and to you shall be faithful and true, and faith to you shall bear for the tenements I hold of you, saving the faith I owe to our sovereign lord the king." "If," says Littleton (*u*), "a man hath several tenancies which he holdeth of several lords, that is to say, every tenancy by homage, then when he doth homage to one of his lords he shall say, at the end of his homage done, 'Saving the faith which I owe to our lord the king and to my other lords.'" None did homage but such as had an estate in fee simple, or fee tail in his own right, or in the right of another. For he who had an estate but for term of life should neither do homage nor take homage (*x*). You will observe that in doing homage the tenant professed to become the lord's man. We consequently find, in many ancient documents, that the tenants of a lord are called *his men*. The lord's men were those who held lands of him in fee simple or fee tail at least, and who, having done him homage, had professed themselves to be, and had in truth become, his own men.

The lord's men.

(*u*) Sect. 89.
(*x*) Littleton, sect. 90.

Another incident of tenure was the oath of fealty, which every tenant, whatever his estate, was bound to take to his lord. This is thus described by Littleton (*y*): "Fealty is the same that *fidelitas* is in Latin, and when a freeholder doth fealty to his lord, he shall hold his hand upon a book and shall say thus, 'Know ye this, my lord, that I shall be faithful and true unto you, and faith to you shall bear for the lands which I claim to hold of you, and that I shall lawfully do to you the customs and services which I ought to do, at the terms assigned, so help me God and his saints:' and he shall kiss the book. But he shall not kneel when he makes his fealty, nor shall make such humble reverence as is aforesaid in homage." "And," Littleton adds (*z*), "there is great diversity between the doing of fealty and of homage, for homage cannot be done to any but the lord himself, but the steward of the lord's court or bailiff may take fealty for the lord." "Also (*a*), a tenant for term of life shall do fealty, and yet he shall not do homage." Fealty.

I beg you to observe the terms of the oath: "I shall lawfully do to you the customs and services which I ought to do." This oath evidently implies that there may be customs incident to the tenure of a freehold estate in fee simple. Some persons seem to suppose that if there be a custom of any sort attached to a tenure, it cannot be freehold. This is a great mistake. Thus, in *Perryman's case* (*b*), it was held to be a good custom of a manor, that every alienation by a freehold tenant of a manor should be presented either at the next court baron, or at some other court baron within a year after the alienation, or at the next court to be held after the expiration of the year, otherwise the same Customs incident to freehold tenure.

(*y*) Sect. 91.
(*z*) Sect. 92.
(*a*) Sect. 93.

(*b*) 5 Co. Rep. 84. See also *Warrick* v. *Queen's College, Oxford*, L. R., 6 Ch. Ap. 716.

should be void. There may, therefore, be customs attached to a freehold tenure, although it is certainly true that this is now not very often the case.

Oath of fealty now obsolete.

I need hardly say that this oath of fealty has now become obsolete, but I am not aware of any act of parliament by which the liability of a tenant to take an oath of fealty to his landlord has been made to cease. Homage was abolished by a statute of 12 Chas. II. c. 24, to which we shall have occasion hereafter to refer. But the freeholders who attend the court baron of their lord are still called the *homage*.

Homage abolished.

The homage.

Suit of court.

Another incident of the tenure of an estate in fee simple was *suit of court*, or the duty of the tenant to attend at the court holden by his lord. For the freeholder who alienated part of his land to another and his heirs, to be holden of himself and his heirs, usually made other similar alienations of other parts of his land to other persons. Provided that he had lands sufficient, there was no limit to the number of freehold tenants which any freeholder might create for himself. I say, provided he had land sufficient, for a limit to these subinfeudations was imposed by Magna Charta as re-issued by King Henry III. You may remember that Magna Charta was first granted by King John. It was three times re-issued, with some amendments, by Henry III. The last re-issue, in the ninth year of his reign, is that printed in the Statutes at Large. The 32nd section of the charter, as issued in the ninth year of the reign of King Henry III., provides that no free man shall henceforth give or sell to any one more of his land than so that, out of the residue of his land, there may be sufficiently done to the lord of the fee the service due to him which belongeth to that fee. But within this limit any freeholder might alienate his lands in fee simple, to be holden of himself, to as many other freeholders as he

Limit to subinfeudation by Magna Charta.

would, all of whom would do him homage, would be his men, would take to him an oath of fealty, and would be bound to attend him at the court to be holden (usually in his mansion or manor house) for regulating the concerns of the body of persons thus constituted.

A manor.

Here we have, in fact, a manor. A manor was made by the owner of an estate in fee carving out other estates in fee to be held by other freeholders as his tenants. A manor consists of demesnes and services: of demesnes, that is, of lands of which the freeholder, now become lord of a manor, is seised in his demesne as of fee; of services, namely, of such yearly rent, called rent service, and other services as he reserved in the grant to his tenants of portions of land, which once were his, to be holden by them and their heirs of him and his heirs. Of the demesne, the lord was seised; of the lands held by free tenants by rent or other services, the tenants themselves were seised, each man in his own demesne as of his own fee. Two free tenants, at least, were necessary to constitute a manor; but there might be as many more as the lord could procure to become his men in the manner before mentioned.

Demesnes and services.

Copyholds.

Copyholds, of which I shall speak hereafter, form no part whatever of the essence of a manor. The lord of a manor may have copyholders or may not; but I am not speaking of them at present. The rights and interests of copyholders are entirely apart from those of the freehold tenants of a manor.

Manors seldom mentioned till time of Edward I.

Manors are mentioned in Domesday, but it is remarkable how little is said in legal documents concerning manors, from the time of William the Conqueror, when Domesday was compiled, down to the time of Edward I., when the Statute of *Quia emptores* was passed. You read of vills or townships, of which I hope to say more in some future course of Lectures. You read also of the Saxon hides of land (familiæ) and yardlands (virgatæ), and of the Norman ploughlands (carucatæ) and ox gangs (bovatæ); but very little occurs about manors until the Statute *Extenta Manerii*, which is said to have been passed in the fourth year of Edward I. And this is hardly to be wondered at, when it is considered that it was in the power of any freeholder, who had sufficient land of his own, to make a manor for himself; and it was in the power of any one of his men, to whom he had granted sufficient land, to be holden by him and his heirs of the grantor and his heirs, himself in like manner to make a sub-manor, by granting out again portions of his own lands to other sub-tenants, to be holden by them and their heirs of him and his heirs. And again one of these sub-tenants might in like manner, and not unfrequently did, create another sub-manor, smaller still, of which he himself was lord, having under him three or four free men, who did him homage, swore to him fealty, paid him rent, and performed services for him, each according to the stipulations in his deed of conveyance. Manors, therefore, were continually being created; and it does not seem to have been necessary that the whole of the land, out of which the freeholder made a manor, should have been holden by him of the same superior lord. Thus a man might have bought lands of a superior lord, A., to hold to himself and his heirs, of A. in fee simple; and he might have bought adjoining lands of another lord, B., to hold to him and his heirs, of B. and his heirs in fee simple; and possibly he might also have acquired other lands of C., a third superior landlord, in the same manner. A tract of land thus acquired he could grant out to other freeholders, to be holden by them of him and his heirs as his tenants; and the services thus created, together with the lands which he held himself, and which constituted his own demesne, would together form one manor, of which he

Sub-manor.

was the lord, and to the court of which his tenants would do suit.

Every man who is now seised in his demesne as of fee of any land holden by him of any lord is still bound to do suit to the court of his lord. But it is provided by the Statute of Merton, 20 Hen. III. c. 10, that every free man, who oweth suit to the court of his lord, may freely make his attorney to do suit for him. Since this statute a freehold tenant is not bound to appear personally at the court of his lord; he may appear by attorney. The attorney, however, must be appointed by deed under seal.

Freeholder is still bound to do suit of court.

May do suit by attorney.

The lord's court thus constituted is called a *court baron*. The word *baron* was often used anciently as meaning merely a free man who held lands. In old law books, such as Comyn's Digest, you will find the law of husband and wife under the head of *baron and feme*. A married woman is also said to be *covert-baron*. In the court baron the suitors were the judges. The steward of the manor was a judicial officer, and formed part of the court, but he had no voice as a judge (*c*). And if any freeholder appeared by attorney, such attorney could not discharge any of the judicial duties which his principal might have done had he appeared in person (*d*). The constitution of these courts was thus remarkably democratic. Every suitor had a voice in every decision. How their jurisdiction arose it is very difficult to say, especially in the case of sub-manors. A grant from the Crown does not seem to have been necessary. But some superior authority was evidently required. And in process of time it became undoubted law that every manor had its court baron as

Court baron.

Steward.

(*c*) *Holroyd* v. *Breare & Holmes*, 2 B. & Ald. 473.
(*d*) 2 Inst. 100.

of common right (*e*). This court was in ancient times usually holden once every three weeks. In this court all suits concerning lands held of the manor might be, and in early times not unfrequently were, determined. But the lord might release his jurisdiction, and in that case the plea might be removed into the county court and from thence to the Court of Common Pleas. The court baron had also cognizance of small matters of debt or damages under 40*s*. But it had no criminal jurisdiction. The criminal court was the *court leet*, a court very differently constituted. The court leet had jurisdiction over all *resiants*, or persons resident within the area of its jurisdiction. The court baron was a court of the freeholders only.

Court leet.

Resiants.

The above three incidents of homage, fealty, and suit of court, belonged to every species of tenure. In ancient times there were two main species of tenure of freehold lands, namely, *tenure by knight's service* and *tenure by free and common socage*. A description of these must be reserved for the next Lecture.

(*e*) 4 Inst. 268.

LECTURE II.

THERE were in ancient times different species of tenures of estates in fee simple. Of these the two most important were *tenure by knight's service* and the tenure by *free and common socage*. The tenure by knight's service was the most frequent and honourable, and also the most burdensome: it involved in the first instance personal military service, which was afterwards commuted into an escuage or money payment. "Escuage," says Littleton (*a*), "is called in Latin *scutagium*, that is, service of the shield, and that tenant which holdeth his land by escuage holdeth by knight's service. And also it is commonly said that some hold by the service of one knight's fee, and some by the half of a knight's fee. And it is said that when the king makes a voyage royal into Scotland, to subdue the Scots, then he which holdeth by the service of one knight's fee ought to be with the king forty days, well and conveniently arrayed for the war; and he which holdeth his land by the moiety of a knight's fee ought to be with the king twenty days; and he which holdeth his land by a fourth part of a knight's fee ought to be with the king ten days; and so he that hath more, more, and he that hath less, less." "But," says Littleton (*b*), "it is not needful for him which holdeth by escuage to go himself with the king, if he will find another able person for him, conveniently arrayed for the war to go with the king. And this seemeth to be good reason. For it may be that he which holdeth by such service is languishing, so as he can neither go nor ride. And also an abbot or other

Knight's service.

Escuage.

(*a*) Sect. 95. (*b*) Sect. 96.

man of religion, or a feme sole, which holdeth by such services, ought not in such case to go in proper person." "And," he adds, "Sir William Herle, then chief justice of the common place, said that escuage shall not be granted but where the king goes himself in his proper person." "And because such tenements came first from the lords it is reason," says Littleton (c), "that they should have the escuage of their tenants. And the lords in such case may distrain for the escuage so assessed, or they in some cases may have the king's writs directed to the sheriffs of the same counties, &c. to levy such escuage for them, as it appeareth by the register. But of such tenants as hold of the king by escuage, which were not with the king in Scotland, the king himself shall have the escuage." Littleton goes on (d) thus:—"Tenure by homage, fealty and escuage is to hold by *knight's service;* and it draweth to it *ward, marriage* and *relief.* For when such tenant dieth, and his heir male be within the age of twenty-one years, the lord shall have the land holden of him until the age of the heir of twenty-one years; the which is called full age, because such heir by intendment of the law is not able to do such knight's service before his age of twenty-one years. And also if such heir be not married at the time of the death of his ancestor, then the lord shall have the *wardship* and *marriage* of him. But if such tenant dieth, his heir female being of the age of fourteen years or more, then the lord shall not have the wardship of the land nor of the body, because that a woman of such age may have a husband able to do knight's service. But if such heir female be within the age of fourteen years and unmarried at the time of the death of her ancestor, the lord shall have the wardship of the land holden of him until the age of such heir female of sixteen years; for it is given by the Statute

Wardship.

Marriage.

(c) Sect. 101.

(d) Sect. 103.

of Westminster 1, c. 22, that, by the space of two years next ensuing the said fourteen years, the lord may tender convenable marriage without disparagement to such heir female. And if the lord within the said two years do not tender such marriage, &c., then she at the end of the said two years may enter and put out her lord. But if such heir female be married within the age of fourteen years in the life of her ancestor, and her ancestor dieth, she being within the age of fourteen years, the lord shall have only the wardship of the land until the end of the fourteen years of age of such heir female, and then her husband and she may enter into the land and oust the lord." A man might hold by knight's service without paying escuage: "as," says Littleton (*e*), "they which hold of their lords by castle-ward, that is to say, to ward a tower of the castle of their lord, or a door, or some other place of the castle, upon reasonable warning, when their lords hear that the enemies will come or are come in England."

Again (*f*), "If a tenant which holdeth of his lord by the service of a whole knight's fee dieth, his heir then being of full age, *scil.* of twenty-one years, then the lord shall have 100*s.* for a *relief;* and of the heir of him who holds by the moiety of a knight's fee, 50*s.*; and of him which holds by the fourth part of a knight's fee, 25*s.*; and so he which more, more, and which less, less." Relief.

"Also (*g*), a man may hold his land of his lord by the service of two knights' fees, and then the heir, being of full age at the time of the death of his ancestor, shall pay to his lord 10*l.* for relief."

In addition to this, the tenant was obliged to *aid* his lord on certain occasions, viz.: To ransom him if taken Aids.

(*e*) Sect. 111.
(*f*) Sect. 112.
(*g*) Sect. 113.

prisoner, to help him in the expense of the knighthood of his eldest son, and in providing a portion for his eldest daughter on her marriage.

Socage.

"Tenure in socage," says Littleton (*h*), "is where the tenant holdeth of his lord the tenancy by certain service for all manner of services, so that the service be not knight's service. As where a man holdeth his land of his lord by fealty and certain rent for all manner of services, or else where a man holdeth his land by homage, fealty and certain rent for all manner of services; for homage by itself maketh not knight's service." "Also (*i*), a man may hold of his lord by fealty only, and such tenure is tenure in socage, for every tenure which is not tenure in chivalry is a tenure in socage." Littleton derives socage from a soke or plough, because the tenants who held by socage ought to come with their ploughs, certain days in the year, to plough and sow the demesnes of the lord. But it is now considered the better opinion that the term *socage* is derived from the Saxon word *soc*, which signifies jurisdiction. Tenants in socage were probably the free suitors of the lord's courts so early as in Saxon times, and held their lands subject to his jurisdiction at the time of the Conquest or soon afterwards. The tenure appears to have been of Saxon rather than of Norman origin.

Escheat.

Knight's service and socage were then the two principal kinds of tenure of freehold lands. A most important incident, common to both tenures, was that of *escheat*, by which, if a tenant died without heirs, the lands escheated or came back again to the lord and his heirs for his own benefit. It was obvious, therefore, that if a tenant granted out part of his lands by subinfeudation, the right of escheat, in case his sub-tenant should die with-

(*h*) Sect. 117. (*i*) Sect. 118.

out heirs, belonged to him and not to his superior lord. So, in case a sub-tenant died leaving an infant heir, his immediate lord, and not the superior lord, had the right of wardship and marriage; and if a sub-tenant died, leaving an heir of full age, his immediate lord, and not the superior lord, had the right to relief. In fact, all the feudal incidents of tenure were far more beneficial to the lord of tenants who were themselves seised of land holden of him, than to lords who had under them other or mesne lords, whose lands had been granted out by them to tenants of their own. The great barons found that, by constant subinfeudation, their power and riches were decreased; their tenants were too apt to become lords themselves, and to enjoy the advantages which they themselves once had. It was principally with a view to putting an end to the inconveniences thus caused, that the great barons, in the time of Edward I., procured the passing of the Statute of *Quia emptores terrarum* (*k*). This statute recites, that for as much as purchasers of lands and tenements of the fees of great men and others have many times heretofore entered into their fees to the prejudice of the lords, the freeholders of such great men and others having sold such lands and tenements to be holden in fee by such purchasers and their heirs of the feoffors and not of the chief lords of the fees, whereby the same chief lords have many times lost their escheats, marriages and wardships of lands and tenements belonging to their fees; which things seemed very hard and extreme unto those great men and other lords, and moreover in this case manifest disinheritance; the king then, at the instance of the great men of the realm, granted, provided and ordained that from thenceforth it should be lawful to every free man to sell at his own pleasure his lands or tenements, or part thereof, so nevertheless that the feoffee should hold

Statute of *Quia emptores.*

(*k*) Stat. 18 Edw. 1, c. 1.

the same lands or tenements of the same chief lord of the fee, and by the same services and customs as his feoffor held them before. And if he sold any part of such lands or tenements to any, the feoffee should hold that immediately of the chief lord, and should be forthwith charged with so much service as pertained or ought to pertain to the said chief lord for such part, according to the quantity of the land or tenements so sold. And so in this case the same part of the service should remain to the lord, to be taken by the hands of the feoffee, for the which he ought to be attendant and answerable to the same chief lord, according to the quantity of the land or tenement sold, for the parcel of the service so due. And it was to be understood that by the said sales and purchases of lands or tenements, or any part thereof, such lands or tenements should in no wise come into mortmain, either in part or in whole, any way by craft or engine, contrary to the form of the statute made thereupon of late (*l*). And it was to be understood that this statute extended only to lands sold to be holden in fee simple. This act is still unrepealed, and it is one which is constantly in operation. How far it is now beneficial may be a question. Wardships, and the right of marriage of infant heirs, and all other feudal benefits of knight's service, have long since been abolished; but the consequence of the existence of this statute is, that if an owner of land suitable for building wishes to convey it in plots to purchasers in fee simple, reserving a rent out of each plot to himself and heirs, he is prevented from doing so directly by this statute. He is obliged to have recourse to the shift of first conveying the plots to the purchaser in fee, to be holden of the same lord, whoever he may be, of whom the vendor formerly held them; and he must then procure each purchaser to grant him a *rent charge* out of the plot so conveyed, to be enjoyed

Remarks on the Statute of *Quia emptores.*

(*l*) Stat. of Mortmain, 7 Edw. 1, st. 2; post, pp. 23, 24.

by the vendor and his heirs for ever. This rent charge is considered in law to be a thing against common right, and is less convenient than a rent service, especially if required to be subdivided or partially released. Again, I see no reason why, in the common case of a squatter unlawfully occupying part of the waste lands of a manor, it should not be competent to the lord to grant him the fee simple of the lands he has occupied, at a perpetual yearly rent, payable to the lord, his heirs and assigns, like the rents payable by his freehold tenants. This is often attempted to be done, in ignorance of the Statute of *Quia emptores*. But I need hardly say that so soon as the squatter has the fee simple of his plot conveyed to him, he becomes tenant in fee, not to the lord who has conveyed it to him, but to the superior lord of whom that lord holds. And the rent attempted to be reserved is not rent service, but rent charge. I think that whenever the time shall come, if ever it should, when our laws shall be rendered suitable to the occasions of modern times, this statute will not, at any rate in its present form, remain upon the Statute Book.

Estate for life.

Estate in tail.

This statute, it will be observed, only applies to estates in fee simple. Hence if I grant part of my lands to a man for his life, he is still my tenant so long as he lives; or if I grant part of my lands to another man and the heirs of his body, he and the heirs of his body are still my tenants so long as the entail endures. If, however, I convey away the whole of my fee simple estate, whether to a man and his heirs, or to one for life with remainder to another in fee, in each case I gain no tenant; but the lord, of whom I held, ceases to be my lord, and becomes at once the lord of the person or persons to whom I may have conveyed my lands.

Statute of Mortmain.

You will observe that the Statute of *Quia emptores* confirmed the Statute of Mortmain passed in the seventh year of Edward I. (*m*). This statute affords conclusive evidence of the subinfeudations, which, as I have said, were continually made until stopped by the passing of the Statute of *Quia emptores*. The Statute of Mortmain is as follows:—

"Where of late it was provided, that religious men should not enter into the fees of any without licence and will of the chief lords, of whom such fees be holden immediately; and afterwards religious men have notwithstanding entered as well into their own fees, as into the fees of other men, appropriating and buying them, and sometime receiving them of the gift of others; whereby the services that are due of such fees, and which at the beginning were provided for defence of the realm, are wrongfully withdrawn, and the chief lords do leese their eschetes of the same: We therefore, to the profit of our realm intending to provide convenient remedy, by the advice of our prelates, earls (barons) and other our lieges, being of our council, have provided, established and ordained that no person, religious or other, whatsoever he be, do presume to buy or sell any lands or tenements, or under the colour of gift or lease, or by reason of any other title, whatsoever it be, to receive from any one, or by any other craft or engine to appropre to himself lands or tenements, under pain of forfeiture of the same, whereby such lands or tenements may anywise come into mortmain."

No person to buy, sell or receive lands into mortmain.

"We have provided also, that if any person, religious or other, do presume any way, by craft or engine, to offend against this statute, it shall be lawful to us, and other immediate chief lords of the fee so aliened, to enter therein within a year from the time of such alienation, and to hold it in fee and inheritance. And if the chief lord immediate be negligent, and will not enter into such fee within the year, then it shall be lawful to

Immediate chief lords may enter.

(*m*) Stat. 7 Edw. 1, st. 2.

the next chief lord immediate of the same fee to enter into the same within half a year next following, and to hold it as before is said; and so every chief lord immediate may enter into such fee if the next lord immediate be negligent in entering into the same fee, as is aforesaid. And if all such lords of such fees being of full age, within the four seas, and out of prison, be negligent or slack in this behalf, we immediately after the year accomplished from the time that such purchases, gifts or other appropriations hap to be made, shall take such lands and tenements into our hand, and shall infeof others therein, by certain services to be therefore done to us for the defence of our realm; saving to the chief lords of the same fees their wards and eschetes, and other services to them due and accustomed."

In default thereof, the next chief lord may enter.

In default thereof, the Crown may take and infeof others of the lands.

The passing of the Statute of *Quia emptores* had the effect of putting a stop to the manufacture of submanors. Hence it follows that every manor must be of a date prior to the passing of this statute; for since this act no man can, by his grant, create a tenant in fee simple to hold of himself. From the time of passing of the Statute of *Quia emptores* down to the restoration of King Charles II., no very great change took place in the tenure of freehold lands held by knight's service. But when Charles II. was restored, the commons took the opportunity of procuring the abolition of the old and burdensome incidents of tenure by knight's service. This was effected by the statute of 12 Charles II. c. 24, by which all tenures by knight's service, of the king or of any other person, and the fruits and consequences thereof, were taken away and discharged; and all tenures of land were turned into free and common socage to all intents and purposes.

Statute 12 Car. 2, c. 24.

The tenure of free and common socage is therefore now the tenure of all lands in this kingdom. It had, as its incidents, in addition to homage which this statute abolished, and fealty and suit of court which were not abolished, no incidents of an oppressive nature. When a tenant died, his heir had to pay one year's quit rent as a *relief* or fine for taking up his ancestor's lands; and this relief still continues, whenever any land holden in fee simple is holden at a yearly rent, payable to the lord of the manor of which it is held.

Socage relief.

The rents anciently reserved in grants in fee have now, in consequence of the change in the value of money, become usually very small; and the result has been, that many ancient manors, the tenants of which themselves made subinfeudations, have been lost for want of care in collecting the small rents, which formed their only income. So that a great quantity of land in this kingdom is now held directly of the Crown, for the simple reason that it is impossible for any intermediate lord to prove that he has the seignory.

Loss of ancient manors.

Littleton's advice.

On this subject the words of Littleton (*n*) are almost prophetic:—"Also, if any will ask why a man may hold of his lord by fealty only for all manner of services, insomuch as when the tenant shall do his fealty he shall swear to his lord he will do to his lord all manner of service due, and when he hath done fealty, in this no other service is due; to this it may be said, that when a tenant holds his land of his lord, it behoveth that he ought to do some service to his lord. For if the tenant nor his heirs ought to do no manner of service to his lord nor his heirs, then, by long continuance of time, it would grow out of memory whether the land were holden of the lord or of his heirs or not; and then will men more often and more readily say that the land is not holden of the lord, nor of his heirs

(*n*) Sect. 130.

than otherwise; and hereupon the lord shall lose his escheat of the land, or perchance some other forfeiture or profit, which he might have of the land. So it is reason that the lord and his heirs have some service done unto them to prove and testify that the land is holden of them." This caution has too frequently been neglected; and there is no doubt that multitudes of manors are now irrecoverably lost. Still there are not a few manors now in existence which have freehold tenants; in fact, as I said before, a manor is not strictly a manor unless it have at least two free tenants. Without these it is only a reputed manor. The recent case of *Warrick* v. *Queen's College, Oxford* (*o*), affords an interesting example of a manor now existing, having a number of freehold tenants, and not a single tenant holding by copy of court roll (a tenancy of which more will be said hereafter). The manor in question is the Manor of Plumstead, in the county of Kent. Four of the freeholders of the manor, on behalf of themselves and the other freehold tenants, filed a bill against Queen's College, the lords of the manor, for the purpose of preventing the enclosure of some of the waste of the manor, and for establishing their right of common on such waste. This right was duly established by the court, and the college were prohibited from enclosing the waste, to the prejudice of the rights of the freehold tenants of the manor. Here we have the ancient feudal tenancy still existing. The tenant is the freeholder: he is seised of his lands in his demesne as of fee; but he holds these lands of the lord of the manor to which these lands belong; he is bound to do him fealty; he is bound to pay him his ancient quit rents. If he dies intestate, his heir is bound to pay one year's quit rent by way of relief. If the lord holds a court, his tenant is bound either to go there in person or to send an attorney

Reputed manor.

Warrick v. *Queen's College.*

(*o*) L. R., 6 Ch. Ap. 716.

duly constituted in his place. The lord is seised in his demesne as of fee of such of the ancient lands of the manor as were never granted out to freehold tenants, but have remained in the manurance or occupation of the lord or his predecessors in title. But he is not seised of the freehold lands which belong to his tenants; over these he has merely an incorporeal right, called his seignory or lordship, to which belong the rents and services reserved by the original grant, namely, fealty, suit of court, and quit rents and reliefs (if any).

There is another case, which was decided by the Court of Common Pleas in the year 1855, which affords a good illustration of our subject. The case is that of

Passingham v. Pitty.

Passingham, appellant, *Pitty*, respondent (*o*). The case arose on the claim of one George Pitty, to vote as a freeholder for the county of Herts, in respect of a tenement which he claimed to be of freehold tenure. His claim was allowed by the revising barrister. The case found that he was seised in fee of a house and land above the annual value of 40*s*., which were conveyed to him by indentures of lease and release, the ordinary mode of assurance in times now gone by. It was shown, by the production of the court rolls of the manor of Digswell, that on 20th of December, 1838, George Pitty acknowledged to hold a house, &c. of the lord of the manor, in the following terms:—

"George Pitty. At this court came George Pitty, of Ashwell aforesaid, miller, and acknowledged in his own proper person to hold to him and his heirs of the lord of this manor by free deed, fealty, suit of court, and a yearly rent of 4*d*., the cottage in High Street, Ashwell, aforesaid, formerly William Balls, &c. (mentioning the former tenants), and he paid to the lord of the said manor 4*d*., for the relief due to him for the

(*p*) 17 Common Bench Reports, 299.

same, but his fealty was respited." It appeared that in the manor of Digswell there were certain tenants who held in precisely the same way as the said George Pitty: the tenants conveyed their estates by ordinary assurance; no special form of deed was required, nor was there any necessity for any express licence from the lord to alien, nor for the enrolment of such assurance in the court rolls, nor for any surrender to be made. Surrender, as we shall see, is the usual mode of alienation of copyholds. Upon the death of, or alienation by, these tenants, the fact ought regularly to be presented at some following court or courts; and it appeared from the court rolls that the lord had, by custom, a right, after three proclamations made, to compel by distress the new owners to come in and acknowledge free tenure. There was a very long argument to show that under these circumstances George Pitty was not a freeholder, entitled as such to vote for the county. "No case," said the learned counsel for the appellant, "can be cited, where a tenant of a manor paying rent to the lord, acknowledging himself tenant to him, and owing fealty and suit of court, is properly a freeholder!" Some of my hearers may, perhaps, suppose that a great deal of what I have been saying is too clear and elementary to form the subject of a public Lecture. But when one sees such a proposition as that I have just quoted, gravely cited by a learned counsel before a court of law, one feels that there is some necessity for insisting on the doctrines which I have endeavoured to explain. So far from the proposition above cited being true, it is the very reverse of the truth. Every freeholder is the tenant, either of some manor, held directly or indirectly from the Crown, or the tenant of the Crown. He is bound to pay his lord such rent, if any, as may have been reserved in the original grant; he is bound to take an oath of fealty; and he is bound to do his lord suit of court. And he is properly called a freeholder; and there is no other designation that I know of by which he could be more properly called. The court, without hearing counsel for the respondent, expressed a clear opinion that the revising barrister was right in holding that George Pitty had a freehold interest; and that his claim was properly allowed. And it would be difficult indeed to see how the court could have come to any other conclusion. His tenure had all the incidents of a freehold tenure, and no distinctive incident of any other tenure. I may remark that the marginal note of the learned reporter contains an error, which it may be as well to notice. His note is, "One who holds in fee land *parcel* of a manor, which by the custom of the manor is conveyed by ordinary assurance, and without any necessity for a licence from the lord, or any enrolment, or surrender and admittance, is a freeholder within the 8th Henry the 6th, chap. 7, *although* at the time of acquiring the estate he acknowledged to hold of the lord by free deed, fealty, suit of court, &c." Without remarking on the word *although*, which seems to imply that the reporter supposed it was contrary to the nature of freehold tenure that a free tenant should hold by fealty and suit of court, I wish to call your attention to the former part of the note, at which it is said, "One who holds in fee land *parcel of a manor*." One who holds in fee of a manor is seised in his demesne as of fee of the lands which he holds. After the grant to his predecessors in title the lands ceased to be *parcel* of the manor, and ought not to be so described. The demesne lands of the lord, including copyholds, if any, and those only, are *parcel* of the manor. The services of the free tenants are also parts of the manor; but their lands are their own, and form no parcel thereof.

There are a few varieties of socage tenures to which it may be sufficient here to refer, as they have not any immediate bearing on the subject of this course of Lectures, which is the relation which the seisin of the freehold bears, among other things, to the tenure of lands. There is the honorary tenure of *grand serjeanty*, and the tenure of *petit serjeanty*. There is the tenure of *gavelkind*, in which the lands descend to all the sons in equal shares, and not to the eldest son only. There is the tenure of *borough English*, in which the lands descend to the youngest son, instead of to the eldest. And there is the tenure of *frankalmoign*, or the tenure of lands belonging to the Church. With respect to all of these I may perhaps venture to refer you to the account contained in my own "Principles of the Law of Real Property" (*q*). But there is also the tenure of *ancient demesne*, with respect to which it may be as well to say a few words. The very learned and able writer of that admirable work, "Blackstone's Commentaries" (*r*), appears to have fallen into the error of supposing that these tenures were altogether copyhold. On this subject I may venture to read a short extract from the Third Report of the Commissioners of the Law of Real Property, which was ordered by the House of Commons to be printed on the 24th of May, 1832 (*s*): "There is great confusion in the law books respecting this tenure (of ancient demesne). All agree that it exists in those manors, and in those only, which belonged to the Crown in the reign of Edward the Confessor and William the Conqueror, and in Domesday Book are denominated *terræ regis*. But the copyholders of these manors are sometimes considered tenants in ancient demesne, and land held in ancient demesne is said to pass by surrender and admittance. This appears to be inaccurate. It is only the freeholders of the manor who are truly tenants in ancient demesne, and land held in ancient demesne passes by common law

Grand serjeanty.

Petit serjeanty.

Gavelkind.

Borough English.

Frankalmoign.

Ancient demesne.

(*q*) Pp. 128—131, 12th ed.

(*r*) Vol. 2, p. 100.

(*s*) Pp. 12, 13.

conveyances, without the instrumentality of the lord. The copyholders in an ancient demesne manor, like other copyholders, are merely to be considered as occupying a part of the lord's demesne, and do not hold of the manor. They form the customary court. The court of ancient demesne, which is analogous to the court baron, is constituted by those who hold in socage of the lord of the manor."

The numerous mesne or intermediate lordships which formerly existed, in most cases between the tenants of the freehold and the Crown as supreme lord, have, as we have seen, dwindled away chiefly for want of evidence of their existence. But in some cases Parliament has assisted in depriving these lords of rights which seemed, from their infrequency and difficulty of proof, to be of no very material value. Thus, in ancient times, if a freehold tenant conveyed any land in mortmain to any corporate body which had perpetual existence and could not leave an heir from whom relief could be obtained, or die without an heir so as to occasion an escheat, such a conveyance was, as we have seen, by the Statute of Mortmain (*t*) a cause of forfeiture to the lord, unless the Crown and every mesne lord gave permission for that purpose.

Conveyance to a corporation.

Stat. 7 & 8 Will. 3, c. 37.

But by stat. of 7 & 8 Will. III. c. 37, it was provided, that it should be lawful for the king, his heirs and successors, when and as often and in such cases as his Majesty, his heirs or successors should think fit, to grant to any person or persons, bodies politic or corporate, their heirs and successors, licence to alien in mortmain, and also to purchase, acquire, take and hold in mortmain, in perpetuity or otherwise, any lands, tenements, rents

(*t*) Stat. 7 Edw. 1, st. 2, ante, pp. 23, 24.

or hereditaments whatsoever, *of whomsoever the same should be holden*. And it was declared that lands, tenements, rents or hereditaments so aliened, or acquired, or licensed, should not be subject to any forfeiture for or by reason of such alienation or acquisition. This act is still in force, and it enables the Crown, by giving licence in mortmain, to deprive the lord, of whom a freehold estate may be immediately holden, of all chance of any escheat, which of course he would possess if the land still remained in the hands of a private person.

Escheat of trust or mortgage estate abolished.

Another statute of the present reign (*u*) takes away from the lord of a freehold tenant the right of escheat in every case in which a tenant may be seised of the land upon any trust or by way of mortgage; except so far as relates to any beneficial interest therein of such trustee or mortgagee. Formerly the corruption of the blood of a tenant, by his being attainted or sentenced to death, formerly for many offences, but ultimately for murder only, was a cause for escheat of his lands to his lord. But by a recent statute (*x*), it is provided that no confession, verdict, inquest, conviction, or judgment of or for any treason or felony or *felo de se*, shall cause any attainder or corruption of blood, or any forfeiture or escheat. And by a still later statute (*y*), on the death of a tenant in fee simple intestate, who is a *bare trustee*, the legal estate in fee vested in him vests now in his legal personal representative for the time being.

Escheat for attainder.

Abolished by stat. 33 & 34 Vict. c. 23.

Bare trustee.

On the whole, therefore, there is very little left to the lord of a freehold tenant, beyond fealty, suit of court, a quit rent, if any was anciently reserved, the

(*u*) Stat. 13 & 14 Vict. c. 60, ss. 15, 19, 46, 47.

(*x*) Stat. 33 & 34 Vict. c. 23, s. 1.

(*y*) Stat. 38 & 39 Vict. c. 87, s. 48.

relief or double quit rent on descent, and the right to escheat in case the tenant (not being a trustee or mortgagee) should die intestate without leaving any heirs. In this case the lord, if he can prove his title against the Crown, will still have the right to resume possession of the lands, and to regain that seisin of the freehold which was parted with by his predecessor in title at the time he made the grant to the predecessor in title of the tenant, whose heirs have failed.

Escheat on failure of heirs.

The doctrine of seisin of the freehold, then, so far as it affects the tenure of an estate in fee simple, is simply this. A tenant in fee holds the feudal possession; he holds his lands in his own demesne; but he holds them of the lord of the manor, to which they belong; for he is seised in his demesne, only as of fee, that is, as of an estate feudally held by him of his superior lord.

Our next subject will be *copyhold tenure*, which you will see is a totally different thing from the freehold tenures which we have hitherto been discussing.

LECTURE III.

We now come to a very ancient and interesting species of tenure, which still exists, and is of much practical importance—namely, the tenure of copyhold. You may remember that the statute of 12 Chas. II. c. 24, abolished the feudal tenure of knight's service with all its burdensome incidents. But there is a clause in this statute (*a*) which provides that that act, nor anything therein contained, shall not alter or change any tenure by copy of court roll or any service incident thereunto. Copyhold.

A manor may or may not have copyhold lands belonging to it. Copyhold lands are such parts of a lord's demesne as, in ancient times, he permitted his villeins or slaves to occupy and till for their own benefit, rendering to him certain rents or other services. If the lord never granted his villeins any such permission, then the manor has no copyholds. Copyholds, therefore, are always *parcel* of the lord's manor; and the lord always was, and is still in law, *seised of them in his demesne as of fee*, and has in law an *actual seisin* of them. He is, in contemplation of law, seised of them in the same manner as he is seised of the lands he actually retains for himself, or as he is seised of the waste lands of the manor, which are still his, though subject to rights of common belonging to the freeholders, and in most cases by custom also to the copyholders of the manor (if any). Parcel of the manor.

Now copyhold land, is land held *by copy of court roll, at the will of the lord, according to the custom of the manor.*

(*a*) Sect. 7.

Copy of court roll.

It is land *held by copy of court roll.* This implies the existence of a court, the proceedings in which are copied out in a roll or book, and copies or extracts of which roll or book are delivered to the tenants, and form their title deeds. There is then *a court* in all cases where the lord of a manor has copyholders. This court is not a court baron, though it is very frequently confounded with it, both courts being often held together (*b*). The court baron is the court of the freeholders, of which, as we have seen, the freeholders are the judges. The court of the copyholders is confined to them; no freeholder has any business there. Its proper designation is the *customary court.* In it the lord, or his steward in his absence, is the judge: the tenants, having anciently been mere slaves, are not intrusted with the privilege of judgment in any cases that may come before them. Again, a copyholder must appear at the court in person. The statute of Henry III., to which we have before referred (*c*), which enables every free man to do suit by attorney, does not apply to copyholders. The suitors who attend are, like the freeholders who attend the court baron (*d*), called the *homage;* they, like freeholders, anciently did homage to their lord; and though the ceremony has been abolished the word remains. Formerly a great deal of business was transacted at the customary court. Every event relating to the alienation or descent of the copyhold lands was presented by the homage for the information of the lord. The presentment was a necessary part of every copyhold assurance. In modern times, however, the holding of customory courts having become very inconvenient, and of very little benefit either to the lord or his tenants, provision was made by parliament by an act in the fourth and fifth years of the Queen (*e*) for the entry in the court rolls of copy-

Customary court.

Copyholder must appear in person.

The homage.

Presentment.

(*b*) See *Doe* d. *Evans* v. *Walker*, 15 Q. B. 28.

(*c*) Stat. 20 Hen. 3, c. 10; *ante*, p. 15.

(*d*) *Ante*, p. 12.

(*e*) Stat. 4 & 5 Vict. c. 35.

hold assurances without the necessity of a presentment to be made of them by the homage. Still, however, the court of the copyholders is occasionally a matter of substance. In some manors the consent of the homage is necessary, in order to enable the lord to grant any portion of the waste of the manor, over which his tenants have rights of common. In this case the homage of the customary court represents the whole body of the copyholders, whilst the homage of the court baron represents the whole body of the freeholders, who are bound by the acts of their representatives.

Grant of waste with consent of homage.

The rolls of the manor were in ancient times separate long pieces of parchment, like the rolls of our courts of law at the present time. They were fastened together at the end, and rolled up into convenient bundles. But in modern times what is called the court roll is neither more nor less than a large book, in which the steward enters every transaction relating to the lands held by every copyholder of the manor. When any transaction takes place relating to copyhold land, a copy of that part of the book in which the transaction is entered is made and signed by the steward, and delivered to the tenant, in whose hands it serves the purpose of a title deed.

Court roll.

Copies of the roll.

Copyholds are held *at the will of the lord.* Originally the copyholders were the lord's villeins or slaves, and the tenure is described by Littleton as tenure in villenage. "Tenure in villenage," says Littleton (*f*), "is most properly when a villein holdeth of his lord, to whom he is a villein, certain lands or tenements according to the custom of the manor or otherwise, at the will of his lord, and to do to his lord villein service, as to carry and re-carry dung of his lord out of the city, or out of his lord's manor, unto the land of his lord, and to spread

The will of the lord.

(*f*) Sect. 172.

the same upon the land and such like. And some free men hold their tenements according to the custom of certain manors by such services. And their tenure also is called tenure in villenage, and yet they are not villeins, for no land holden in villenage, or villein land, nor any custom arising out of the land, shall ever make a free man villein."

Custom of the manor.

I need hardly say that there are no villeins at the present day, nor have been in this country for some centuries. Copyholds, which were anciently holden by villeins, are now holden by free men. The lands are, however, still expressed to be held at the will of the lord, although for a long time the lord practically has had no will in the matter; for copyholds are holden not only at the will of the lord, but also *according to the custom of the manor*, and the custom of holding ultimately prevailed against the will of the lord. Those who had thus holden lands for a long time were ultimately decided by the courts of law to have the right to hold them still, provided they did the services which were due in respect of the lands according to the custom of the manor. In the 77th section of Littleton's Tenures it is said that, "although that some such tenants have an inheritance according to the custom of the manor, yet they have but an estate but at the will of the lord, according to the course of the common law. For it is said that if the lord do oust them, they have no other remedy but to sue to their lords by petition; for if they should have any other remedy, they should not be said to be the tenants at will of the lord according to the custom of the manor. But the lord cannot break the custom, which is reasonable in these cases." And it is added in some editions, "But Brian, chief justice, said that his opinion hath always been, and ever shall be, that if such tenant by custom, paying his services, be ejected by the lord, he shall have an action of trespass against him.

(Hilary Term, 21 of Edward IV.) And so was the opinion of Danby, chief justice, in the 7 of Edward IV. For he saith that tenant by the custom is as well inheritor to have his land, according to the custom, as he which hath a freehold at the common law." The opinion of Brian and Danby is now undoubted law, although it seems from the above extract that, even in Littleton's time, there was some question about it. Copyholds are still at law merely estates at will, but they are estates at will established by the custom of the manor, which has come to control the will of the lord. So that the copyholder, provided he pays his rent and performs his services, cannot be turned out of the tenement he holds. For custom is the life of copyholds. Although custom has thus acquired the force of law, and now prevents the lord of the manor from turning out his copyholders, it has not taken from the lord some of the incidents which belong to an estate in fee simple in possession. I have said that the lord has an actual seisin of all the copyholds of his manor. In consequence of this actual seisin it is that the lord, and not the copyhold tenant, is entitled to all *timber* growing on copyhold lands, and also to all *mines* and *minerals* under the same. The lord is entitled to all *timber* growing on the lands; but the tenant is by Timber. custom entitled to the possession of the lands, including in it the possession of the timber. So that the lord is in this dilemma: the timber is his, but he cannot get at it without his tenant's leave. The consequence is that timber is not often to be seen on lands of copyhold tenure. There is no encouragement to a tenant to plant timber, which, when grown up, will not be his own; and the lord cannot plant it, because if he were to attempt to do so, he would infringe on the possession of his copyholder. Again, *mines and minerals* under copyhold lands Mines. belong to the lord. He is seised of the surface, and the seisin of the surface carries with it the seisin of everything below the surface; but here, as in the case of timber, the copyholder has possession of the surface, and having possession of the surface, he has, in intendment of law, possession of everything that is below the surface. The lord, therefore, cannot enter upon a copyhold tenement and work his mines without infringing on his tenant's possession, and the tenant cannot work them without taking his lord's property. Unless, therefore, both can agree, the mines must remain unworked and the minerals must sleep underground a useless slumber (*g*).

Waste.

Another result of the fact that a copyhold tenant has merely possession, grown by custom into a right, is this:—That a copyhold tenant cannot commit any *waste* upon the lands he holds. He is bound to keep all buildings in repair, and to maintain his tenement, as though in fact it were his lord's and not his own. In this he differs from a tenant of freehold lands in fee simple. A tenant in fee simple may commit what waste or destruction he pleases; and the lord of the fee has no voice in the matter. He may pull down houses, turn arable into pasture, or even into waste land, open mines, cut down timber, and in fact make what destruction he pleases, without let or hindrance, either from his superior lord or any other person. But a copyholder cannot do so. His estate was originally an estate at will; and the custom, whilst it has confirmed him in his possession, has not deprived the lord of the right to have the tenements properly kept up, just as if they were his own.

Lease.

Another result of this state of circumstances is, that a copyholder cannot grant a *lease* of his copyhold lands, beyond the term of one year, without his lord's licence; unless indeed there should be, as there occasionally is, an especial custom for that purpose. A tenant at will

(*g*) *Eardley* v. *Granville*, L. R., 3 Ch. Div. 826.

cannot create, out of his tenancy at will, a larger estate than that he himself has. A copyholder, therefore, notwithstanding the certainty of his own possession, cannot grant a lease of his copyhold lands for any longer term than one year, without running the risk of a forfeiture to the lord of his copyhold tenement. If the lord grants his licence to a copyholder to make a lease, the lease is said to take effect in law out of the seisin of the lord: it is the lord in fact who, being seised in fee, grants the lease; although he does it by means of a licence accorded to his copyhold tenant. It follows that a lord, who is only tenant for life of a manor, cannot grant to a copyholder of the manor a licence to lease his copyhold tenement for any period to endure beyond the lord's own life. In this respect the power of the lord contrasts strongly with his power to make a copyhold grant, which, as we shall see, taking effect by custom only, can be made to endure so long as the custom warrants, by any lord of the manor, however limited his estate. Licence.

Notwithstanding all these circumstances, copyhold tenure is often a very advantageous one. The fact of the title being registered in the books of the manor is often looked upon, and I think with justice, as a great advantage. The tenant is secure in his possession so long as he does his services; and he may dispose of the lands he holds by copy, in such a way as to create out of them very nearly the same kind of estates and interests as may be held in freehold land.

First grant that the lord is seised in fee, and that the copyholder in law is but a tenant at will; then remember that, though tenant at will, a copyholder has in truth a permanent estate, and you will next see that there may be estates in copyholds similar to, though not by any means the same as, estates in freehold land. There may be *quasi freehold estates* in copyhold lands. There may be an estate for life; there may be, if the custom warrant it, an estate tail; and there may be a customary estate in fee simple; exactly in analogy to similar estates holden in freehold lands. There may be an *estate for life;* and in some manors the custom does not permit of any larger estate than an estate, sometimes for one life, sometimes for two or three lives, one after the other. In this case when the lives drop, fresh lives must be put in. By custom a tenant may have a perpetual right of renewal, that is, a perpetual right of adding new lives as the old ones drop. Or a renewal may, by the custom of the manor, be at the pleasure of the lord. When the fine to be paid to the lord for renewal is fixed, the renewal is at the tenant's option; when the fine is arbitrary, the renewal is at the lord's option.

Estate for life.

Fines for renewal.

Estates tail.

By the custom of some manors, customary estates tail are permitted analogous to those held in freehold lands. By the custom of other manors, estates in tail are prohibited. On the subject of entails I propose to say more when I come to that branch of my subject which relates to the seisin of the freehold as it affects settlement.

Fee simple.

By the custom of most manors, where there are copyhold tenants, the copyholders may have a customary estate in fee simple, or an estate to the tenant and his customary heirs. The customary heirs of a tenant are very frequently the same persons as would be the heirs of a person holding an estate in fee simple in freehold lands. But the customs of many manors are peculiar in this respect. In some, the lands descend to the youngest son, according to the custom of borough English. This is the case in many manors in Sussex. In others, the lands descend to all the sons, according to the custom of gavel-kind. And in some manors the customs of inheritance are still more peculiar. But all the estates thus created are only *quasi* estates; they are analogous to freehold estates, but they are not freehold, because the freehold is in the lord.

Now it is impossible, in the course of a single Lecture, to give you the whole of the law of copyholds, nor is it at all desirable that I should. I wish to impress upon your minds the principles upon which the law of copyholds is founded. The alienation of copyholds takes place in a very different manner from the alienation of freeholds, to which I have already adverted, but of which I shall speak more particularly when I come to the seisin of the freehold as it affects conveyance. Where any portion of a manor is subject by custom to copyhold tenure, it is competent to the lord of the manor to grant out such portion of the lands to a tenant Grants. for such estate as is warranted by the custom, usually to the tenant and his customary heirs, to be holden, by the tenant and his heirs, of the lord and his heirs, for a customary estate in fee simple. The Statute of *Quia emptores* (*h*), to which we have before adverted, prevents, as you may recollect, the subinfeudation of freehold lands; but this statute does not apply to copyholds; it does not therefore prevent the lord of a manor, when the custom sanctions it, from granting lands to be holden, by a tenant by copy of court roll, for a customary estate in fee simple, of the lord and his heirs. But, in this case, the lord still remains seised in fee of what he has thus granted; the tenement still remains *parcel* of his own demesne at law; his tenant is only a tenant at will, but by custom he has the right to remain, and his heirs after him, so long as he and they perform the services reserved in the grant.

It is in fact custom, and custom only, which enables Custom.

(*h*) Stat. 18 Edw. 1, c. 1; *ante*, p. 21.

the lord of a manor, in which parcel of the demesne is subject to customary tenure, to make a grant thereof. The grant takes effect by the custom, and by the custom only. It is quite irrespective of the estate of the lord in the manor:—thus, if the custom authorizes the grant of land for a customary estate in fee simple, such a grant may be made by the lord for the time being, however small may be his estate in the manor. Thus a tenant for life of the manor may, as lord, according to the custom, grant lands which are subject to the custom to hold by copy in fee simple. So even a tenant for years of the manor may make a similar grant, if the custom of the manor warrants such a grant. It is not from the estate of the lord that such a grant takes effect, but by virtue of the custom, and that only.

Swayne's case. A curious illustration of this principle occurred in an old case in the time of James I., called *Swayne's case*, which is reported in the 8th volume of Lord Coke's Reports (*i*). Richard Swayne, Esq., brought an action of trespass against Walter Becket for lopping ten oaks and fifteen ashes, &c., at Hannington in the county of Wilts. The case was this. Queen Elizabeth was seised of the manor of Hannington in the county of Wilts in fee, in the right of her Duchy of Lancaster; and the said oaks and ashes so lopped were growing upon a yard and half of land, parcel of the same manor, and copyhold land of the manor. Queen Elizabeth demised the same manor to John Wolly (except all woods, underwoods, trees and timber), to hold for twenty-one years. Wolly assigned his interest to John Plumer and others. Afterwards the Queen died; and King James, by letters patent under the duchy seal, granted to Richard Swayne and others the reversion of the premises, to hold to them and their heirs; to whom the

(*i*) 8 Rep. 63.

lessees attorned. Afterwards the other grantees released to Richard Swayne and his heirs; so that he became sole lord of the manor, subject only to the lease; in which lease you will see that the timber was excepted. Afterwards, at a court held by the lessees, 17th October, in the third year of the reign of King James, their steward granted, by copy of court roll, to Walter Becket, the defendant, a house and the said yard and half of land, upon which the said oaks and ashes were growing, for the term of his life, according to the custom of the manor. Within the manor there was a custom that every copyhold tenant for life hath used to take all trees growing upon his copyhold lands to be employed for fuel in his copyhold house, and for bounds and fences and other necessary reparations to be made in and upon the customary lands and tenements. And the defendant did lop the said trees upon his copyhold, and employed them for bounds and fences in and upon his copyhold lands and tenements. And the doubt was that, forasmuch as the said lessees held the court by virtue of the said lease of the manor (out of which lease the said trees were excepted), whether the defendant, to whom they by their steward granted the said tenement by copy, might lop the said trees, which, by the said exception, were divided from the said lease. And it was resolved by the whole court that, notwithstanding the severance by the exception, and notwithstanding the defendant came in by a voluntary grant of the lords, for life, and not by surrender, yet such grantee by copy should have *estovers* (that is, the right of cutting trees for fuel and repairs, &c.). "For the estate of the copyholder who comes in by voluntary grant is," the court said, "not derived out of the estate or interest of the lord of the manor, for the lord of the manor is but as an instrument to make the grant; but the custom of the manor, after the grant made, establishes and makes it firm to the grantee. So that, although the grant be new, yet the title of the copyholder is ancient, and so ancient that, by force of custom, it exceeds the memory of man. And therefore neither for infancy, non sane memory, coverture nor other such disabilities, neither in respect of exile, baseness or uncertainty of the interests or estates of the lords (as at will or upon condition, &c.), the grants by copy shall not be avoided, because they claim in, by force of a good and ancient custom, which hath no disability of person, or defect of perfect interest." It was even resolved (*k*), that "when the copyholders for life, according to the custom, have used to have common in the wastes of the lord of the manor, or estovers in his woods, or any other profit *apprender* in any part of the manor, and afterwards the lord aliens the wastes or woods to another in fee, and afterwards grants certain copyhold houses and lands for lives, such grantees shall have common of pasture or common of estovers, &c., notwithstanding the severance. For the title of the copyholder is paramount the severance; and the custom unites the common or estovers, which are but accessories or incidents, as long as the house and lands, being principal, are maintained by the custom; which customary appurtenances are not appertaining to the estate of the lord; for he is the owner of the freehold and inheritance of all the manor; but they are appertaining to the customary estate of the copyholder after the grant made unto him; which profit *apprender*, being due by custom to the copyhold tenement (notwithstanding the feoffment or fine, &c. (that is, the conveyance), of the waste or woods made by the lord), remains and is preserved by the custom, which is, as hath been said, the title of the copyholder, and is paramount the severance. But if the copyholder had derived his interest from the estate of the lord, then clearly by the feoffment or fine, &c. of the lord, all those

(*k*) Pp. 63 b, 64 a.

who after claim by him shall be barred of any profit *apprender* in the same waste or woods."

Destruction of the custom.

A grant of copyholds takes effect then by custom, and by custom only. And if land, subject to the custom of grant by copy, falls into the hands of the lord, and he, instead of granting it by copy, conveys it by any common law assurance, he puts an end at once to the custom, and disables both himself and every future lord who claims under him from again granting the tenements out to be holden by copy of court roll. But if the lord is only tenant for life, the custom will revive after his decease.

Surrender and admittance.

When a copyholder wishes to alienate his land, he does so by *surrendering* his tenement into the hands of his lord to the use of the person in whose favour the alienation is intended to be made. The lord then *admits* the alienee as his tenant, and from that time the alienee becomes the copyholder in the place of the alienor. As a copyholder has not the freehold estate in fee simple, he cannot convey his copyholds by any of the means by which a tenant in fee simple may convey his freeholds. Surrender and admittance are the established modes for the alienation of copyholds. The surrender was formerly required to be presented, but, as I said before, presentment is now unnecessary. All that needs be done is to get the steward to enter the surrender on the court rolls of the manor after the surrender has been made. The surrenderor, or the person who has made the surrender, still continues the lord's copyhold tenant until the admission of the surrenderee. After the surrenderee has been admitted, he becomes the lord's copyhold tenant in the place of the surrenderor. Anciently, no doubt, it was a favour on the part of the lord to admit the surrenderee of his copyhold tenant. The copyholder gave up his tenement into the hands of the lord, hoping that the lord would admit in his place the person named in the surrender. But ultimately the custom gave the surrenderee a right to be admitted, and it compelled the lord to admit him. The lord is now looked upon as holding, in this respect, an office purely ministerial, and he may be compelled by mandamus from the Queen's Bench Division of the High Court, or by injunction from the Chancery Division, to admit the surrenderee. On admission, the lord is usually entitled to a fine, but the fine is not due till after the admission, and the lord must first admit a surrenderee and then demand his fine.

Admittance compulsory on the lord.

Fine.

In theory, then, a copyholder is but a tenant at will, but practically he is now independent of the lord of the manor, parcel of whose demesne he holds by copy.

One of the great difficulties of the student of the English Law of Real Property is the number of systems of law he has to master. Having learned all about estates in freeholds, he finds, when he comes to copyholds he has to learn a number of *quasi estates*, not the same in every respect yet generally similar. If it were possible entirely to get rid of copyholds, the law of real property would be greatly simplified. A great deal has been done in that direction. Provisions have been made for the *enfranchisement* of copyhold lands, or the turning them into freehold tenure, either voluntarily, by agreement between the lord and tenant, or compulsorily at the instance of either. It is not necessary that I should here set out all the acts of parliament which have been passed for that purpose. You will find them in any treatise on copyhold law. They are also mentioned in the chapter on Estates in Copyholds, in my "Principles of the Law of Real Property" (*l*). My main object has

Enfranchisement.

(*l*) Pp. 368—371, 12th ed.

been to show you the great differences which exist between freehold tenure and copyhold tenure. The same lord of the same manor may have both freehold tenants and copyhold tenants, but they are two very distinct classes; the freeholders hold and possess their own lands in fee, subject only to the services due to their lord. The lord is seised in fee of the copyhold lands, which remain parcel of his demesne, subject only to the rights which custom has given to his copyhold tenants.

There is another species of tenure, of which it is desirable to say a few words, viz. what is commonly called *customary freehold*. *Customary freeholds* are merely a privileged and superior kind of copyholds. The tenants of these lands hold by copy of court roll according to the custom of the manor; but they are not said to hold at the will of the lord. This tenure prevails chiefly in the north of England, where it is not unfrequently known by the name of *tenant right*. It is now well settled that the freehold of all tenements, held by this tenure, is in the lord, and not in the tenant. You have seen that, in the case of pure copyholds, the expression *at the will of the lord* has now become merely complimentary, and nothing more. Copyholds anciently were held at the will of the lord; now they are held independently of his will. But, in the case of customary freeholds, the phrase appears to have been long dropped. Still the holders of such tenements are essentially copyholders. Their tenements are parcel of the manor; they have no right to work the minerals, nor to cut the timber on their tenements, nor to grant leases thereof without licence. For these acts would infringe upon the freehold, which remains vested in the lord of the manor. You will find the law upon this subject well laid down by Vice-Chancellor Wood, now Lord Hatherley, in the

Customary freeholds.

Tenant right.

case of the *Duke of Portland* v. *Hill* (m), and by the present Master of the Rolls, in the case of *Eardley* v. *Granville* (n).

The subject of my next Lecture will be the *seisin of the freehold as it affects descent.*

(m) L. R., 2 Eq. 765.

(n) L. R., 3 Ch. Div. 826.

LECTURE IV.

THE subject of the present Lecture is the seisin of the freehold as it affects DESCENT.

Descent, as you know, is that which happens with respect to land of freehold tenure, when the owner thereof dies without a will. The lands are then popularly said to descend to his heir-at-law. This expression, though true in a general way, is not always strictly true in a legal sense. The law with respect to descent underwent great alterations at the time when several measures were passed for the improvement of the law. The act 3 & 4 Will. IV. c. 106, was passed for the amendment of the law of inheritance, and this act, with some amendments since made, is now the law by which descent is regulated. Descent.

The subject of descent is not an easy one; it is one over which not a few learned persons have stumbled; and it seems to me very desirable that you should first obtain a clear idea of what the law of descent was before the passing of that act, in order to enable you the better to understand the law as regulated by that act.

Under the new act, as we shall hereafter see, all descent is traced from the purchaser; but under the law as it stood before the act, descent was traced from the *person who was last seised* of the land. If the person last seised was himself the purchaser, of course it made no matter; but if the person last seised was not the Person last seised.

purchaser, but had become entitled himself, as the heir of some other person, then the heir under the old law was in some cases different from the heir under the present law; and the difference depended upon the *seisin of the freehold*, as I shall attempt to explain.

The rules or canons of descent under the old law were as follows:—

Old canons of descent.

1. Hereditaments shall lineally descend to the issue of the person who last died actually seised, *in infinitum;* but shall never lineally ascend.
2. The male issue shall be admitted before the female.
3. Where there are two or more males in equal degree, the eldest only shall inherit, but the females altogether.
4. The lineal descendants, *in infinitum*, of any person deceased shall represent their ancestor; that is, shall stand in the same place as the person himself would have done had he been living.
5. On failure of lineal descendants, or issue of such person, the inheritance shall descend to his collateral relations, being of the blood of the first purchaser; subject to the three preceding rules.
6. The collateral heir of such person must be his next collateral kinsman of the whole blood.
7. In collateral inheritances, the male stock shall be preferred to the female (*i. e.*, kindred derived from the blood of the male ancestors, however remote, shall be admitted before those from the blood of the female, however near); unless where the lands have in fact descended from a female.

These canons require explanation.

1st rule.

The 1*st rule* was that hereditaments should lineally descend to the issue of the person who last died *actually* *seised, in infinitum;* but should never lineally ascend. An actual seisin, therefore, was, under the old law, absolutely necessary, in order to make an heir-at-law himself the stock of descent, in the event of his decease intestate; that is, in order to enable his own heir-at-law to claim the property by descent. If a person, to whom lands had descended, had not acquired an *actual seisin*, but had only a seisin in law, then the hereditaments did not descend to his heir, but to the heir of the person who was last seised. The maxim was *Non jus sed seisina facit stipitem.* *Seisina facit stipitem.*

Mr. Watkins, in his Essay on the Law of Descent (*a*), thus writes:—"In case the ancestor takes by purchase he may be capable of transmitting the property so taken to his own heirs, without any actual possession in himself. But if the ancestor himself takes by descent, it is absolutely necessary, in order to make him the stock or terminus, from whom the descent should now run, and so enable him to transmit such hereditaments to his own heirs, that he acquire an *actual seisin* of such as are corporeal, or what is equivalent thereto in such as are incorporeal, or that he exert some act of ownership over such as are in reversion or remainder expectant upon an estate of freehold."

"Immediately," he goes on (*b*), "on the death of the ancestor (whether such ancestor had taken by descent or by purchase), or the intermediate person to whom the estate devolved (whether such person had an actual seisin or not), the law casts the estate upon the heir. And as he has thus the right, it gives him also a presumed possession or seisin; for I speak now of estates in possession. On the death of the ancestor, as the possession would be otherwise vacant, the law supposes or presumes it to be in the heir; and this presumptive

(*a*) P. 32, 4th ed. (*b*) P. 34.

possession or seisin is what is termed a possession or *seisin in law*."

"And we must be careful to remark that this possession or seisin in law in the heir is, as we have stated it, no more than supposed or presumed; for if there be an actual possession or seisin, either by right or by wrong, in any other person, such actual possession or seisin rebuts the presumption of a seisin in the heir."

"If, on the death of such ancestor, the hereditaments descending were in lease for years to any, then the possession of the lessee for years gives not a seisin or possession in law, but a seisin or possession in deed to such heir."

Again (*c*), "The person in the corporeal possession of the freehold, who is in the perception of the profits, who has the actual possession, has the seisin in deed; the person who has a right of property in the premises, and also a title to enter immediately into them (when the possession is vacant), has a seisin in law. In the former case the possession is already full and therefore excludes a presumption; but in the latter, it being vacant, the law presumes it to be in him who has right. But if the actual possession be in one person, and another has a title to enter during such possession, he has but *a right*, by reason of the actual possession being in such person."

Abatement.

Again (*d*), "If on the death of the ancestor a stranger enters before the heir, and in legal language *abates*, then the actual possession of the abator, though by wrong, shall rebut the seisin or possession in law of the heir. So had the ancestor himself been disseised and died before a subsequent entry, the actual seisin would be in such disseisor, and the heirs have but a right."

(*c*) P. 38. (*d*) P. 40.

You may remember that, in my first Lecture, I endeavoured to illustrate the difference between seisin in law and an actual seisin, by putting the case of a man seised in fee of two farms—Whiteacre and Blackacre (*e*). Whiteacre he kept in his own possession, Blackacre he let to a yearly tenant. He then died intestate; and I observed that his heir-at-law was not actually seised of Whiteacre, the possession of which became vacant on his ancestor's death, until he entered and took possession; but of Blackacre he was, in contemplation of law, actually seised from the moment of his ancestor's death; because the possession of a yearly tenant was looked upon as the landlord's own possession. This doctrine was usually illustrated by an example; from the first words of which it was called the doctrine of *possessio fratris*. The whole phrase was thus—"Possessio fratris de feudo simplici facit sororem esse hæredem"—The possession of the brother of an estate in fee simple makes his sister to be heir. This is spoken with reference to the following state of circumstances:—A man dies intestate, leaving a son and a daughter by his first wife, and a son by his second wife; if the eldest son then entered and took possession, and so became actually seised, he became the stock of descent, and the land descended to his heir-at-law. Now his heir-at-law was his sister of the whole blood; and under the old law his brother of the half blood never could inherit the land as his heir. If, however, the eldest son died before entry (the possession being vacant, and not being held by any tenant, whose occupation would give him actual seisin), then the land would descend to the next heir of the person who was last actually seised. Now the person who was last actually seised was the father, and his next heir was his second son by his second wife, and not

Possessio fratris.

(*e*) *Ante*, p. 5.

his daughter by his first wife; the rule being, as we have seen, that the males were always to be preferred to the females. The son, therefore, as male, took before the daughter, who was a female. In this case, therefore, you see that the possession of the elder son made his sister to be his heir; his want of possession made his brother of the half blood to be not his heir, but the heir of his father, who was the person last actually seised.

How actual seisin gained. Entry.

Now actual seisin was obtained, when the possession was vacant, by the entry of the heir upon the property. If the heir was an infant, it was gained by the entry or possession of his guardian or lord (*f*). So, as we have seen, it was gained by the possession of the ancestor's lessee for years. An actual seisin of the demesne lands of a manor, which were subject to the custom of copyhold, and were in the possession of tenants by copy of court roll, was gained by the possession of such tenants; for copyholds were originally, as we have seen, and yet are in the eye of the law, only tenancies at will, the freehold remaining in the lord. On the death of the lord therefore intestate, his heir becomes *actually seised*, in point of law, of all the lands in the manor which are in the possession of his copyhold tenants. It was further unnecessary that the heir-at-law, when the possession was vacant, should enter in his own person; for the entry of an indifferent person in his name and to his use was sufficient. If the heir gained an actual seisin by any of the above methods, then the land descended to his heir, and not to the heir of his ancestor.

Possession of lessee for years.

Possession of copyhold tenants.

Entry of coparcener or tenant in common.

An actual seisin might also have been obtained, in the case of a coparcener or tenant in common, by the entry of the other coparcener or tenant in common, or

(*f*) *Thomas* v. *Thomas*, 2 Kay & J. 79.

of any of the others, if more than one; for, under the old law, the possession of one coparcener, joint tenant, or tenant in common, was considered to be the possession of all. But the Act for the Limitation of Actions and Suits (*g*), which was passed in the same session of parliament as the Act to amend the Law of Inheritance, provides (*h*), both retrospectively and prospectively, that when any one or more of several persons entitled to any land or rent as coparceners, joint tenants or tenants in common, shall have been in possession or receipt of the entirety, or more than his or their undivided share or shares of such land, or of the profits thereof, or of such rent, for his or their benefit, or for the benefit of any person or persons other than the person or persons entitled to the other share or shares of the same land or rent, such possession or receipt shall not be deemed to have been the possession or receipt of or by such last-mentioned person or persons, or any of them.

Entry of younger brother or sister.

So the entry of a younger brother or sister, even although he or she were but of the half blood, was in law considered to be the possession of the eldest brother, or of the other sisters, as the case might be. But the same statute (*i*) enacts (*k*), that when a younger brother or other relation of the person entitled as heir to the possession or receipt of the profits of any land, or to the receipt of any rent, shall enter into the possession or receipt thereof, such possession or receipt shall not be deemed to be the possession or receipt of or by the person entitled as heir.

Copyholds.

We have seen that there may be customary estates in fee simple in copyhold lands (*l*). These lands descend, on the decease of the ancestor intestate, to his next heir,

(*g*) Stat. 3 & 4 Will. 4, c. 27.
(*h*) Sect. 12.
(*i*) Stat. 3 & 4 Will. 4, c. 27.
(*k*) Sect. 13.
(*l*) *Ante*, p. 42.

according to the custom of the manor to which the copyholds belong. The customary heir cannot, strictly speaking, gain an actual seisin of the copyhold lands which have descended to him, for, as we have seen, the actual seisin is in the lord. But by entry upon the descended lands he might gain a possession sufficient, under the old law, to make him the stock of descent, whether he had been formally admitted as his lord's tenant or not; for, under the old law, it was the entry of the heir, and not his admission, which made a *possessio fratris* of copyholds (*m*).

Incorporeal hereditaments.

If the hereditaments claimed were incorporeal, such as a rent-charge in fee, or an advowson in gross, that is, a perpetual right of presentation to an ecclesiastical benefice, not appendant or appurtenant to any manor, then actual receipt of the rent, or actual presentation to the advowson, were requisite in order to make an heir-at-law, on whom they had descended, himself the stock of descent. But if the advowson were appendant or appurtenant to a manor, then actual seisin of the manor would give actual seisin also of the advowson as its appendancy (*n*).

The latter clause of the first canon was that hereditaments should never lineally ascend, that is, they should never go by inheritance to the father or any other lineal ancestor of the stock of descent. This rule, as we shall see, has been abolished by the Act to amend the Law of Inheritance.

2nd rule.

The *2nd rule* seems sufficiently clear: That the male issue shall be admitted before the female, viz. all the sons before any daughter, all the brothers before any sister, all the uncles before any aunt, and so on.

(*m*) *Doe* d. *Hamilton* v. *Clift*, 12 Ad. & Ell. 566.

(*n*) Watkins on Descents, 67—69, 4th ed.

The *3rd rule* is generally well known, viz. this: That where there are two or more males in equal degree, the eldest only shall inherit. Thus, if a man die intestate, leaving two sons, his elder son only shall inherit his lands, to the exclusion of the younger son. But the females inherit altogether. If a man dies and leaves two daughters, they will inherit together. Each will take a moiety as co-heir with the other. Those who inherit as co-heirs are called coparceners. 3rd rule. Coparceners.

The *4th rule* is a very important one, and requires a little explanation. The lineal descendants, *in infinitum*, of any person deceased shall represent their ancestor; that is, shall stand in the same place as the person himself would have done had he been living. If, therefore, a freeholder dies intestate, having had an eldest son who died in his lifetime, leaving an only daughter who survives her grandfather, and there is also another son of the intestate living at his decease, the land shall not descend to the son who survives, although he is a male, and so would be preferred to a female in equal degree. But the daughter of the eldest son shall come in, by representation of her father, and inherit the whole of the estate. She is the lineal descendant of her father, and, as such, represents him and stands in his place. She takes precisely as he himself would have done had he been living. 4th rule.

This rule is well illustrated by the case of *Clements* v. *Scudamore* (*o*). It was an action of ejectment tried in the Court of King's Bench. The jury found this special verdict: J. S. had issue five sons, the youngest of which died in the lifetime of J. S., leaving issue a daughter (the lessor of the plaintiff), after which J. S. purchased the lands in question, which were copyhold and of the *Clements* v. *Scudamore*.

(*o*) 1 P. Wms. 63.

nature of borough English, descendible by the custom to the youngest son and his heirs; J. S. died seised, that is, he had a *quasi* seisin, for the actual seisin of the freehold was, as you know, in the lord of the manor. The fourth son entered, upon which the question was, whether the fourth son or the daughter of the fifth son should inherit these lands. And after several arguments at bar, C. J. Holt delivered the opinion of the whole court in favour of the daughter, viz. that she ought to inherit these lands *jure repræsentationis.*

"Wherever," he said, "this custom has obtained, the youngest son is there placed in the room of the eldest, who inherits by the common law; and there is no difference in the course of descents, but that the custom prefers the youngest son and the common law the eldest; and therefore, as by the common law the issue of the eldest son, female as well as male, do, *jure repræsentationis*, inherit before the other brothers, so, by the same reason, when this custom has transferred the right of descent from the eldest to the youngest son, it shall also, by the like representation, carry it to the daughter of the youngest son: and there is no ground to make any difference betwixt a descent by this custom and by the common law."

5th rule.

The *5th rule* was, that on failure of lineal descendants or issue of the person who last died actually seised, the inheritance should descend to his collateral relations, *being of the blood of the first purchaser*, subject to the three preceding rules. Thus, if a man died without issue, his eldest brother was his heir-at-law; or if his eldest brother had died in his lifetime, leaving a daughter, then that daughter, by right of representation of her father, was his heir-at-law. If he left no brother nor descendants of any brother, then his sisters became his co-heirs as coparceners in equal shares. Or if any sister had died in his lifetime leaving issue, then the issue of such sister took by representation their mother's share. But there was this important limitation, that the inheritance descended to the collateral relations of the person last seised, *being of the blood of the first purchaser*. Thus, if a woman had land by purchase, and married, the issue of the marriage would, on her decease intestate, be her heir-at-law. In case she had had an only son, who survived her and then died intestate and without issue, and without gaining an actual seisin, then she herself would be the stock of descent, and the lands would descend to her heir. If, however, her son gained an actual seisin, and then died without issue, the lands would descend to his heir, because he died actually seised; but they would descend to his heir *ex parte maternâ*, on the part of his mother, because of the 5th rule. By this rule the inheritance was to descend to his collateral relations *being of the blood of the first purchaser*. His father's brother, therefore, could not be heir of this estate; for the inheritance would descend to the heir on the part of his mother; and the first person to inherit would be the eldest brother of his mother; and in default of such eldest brother, then the issue of such eldest brother, as representing him; or, in default of such issue, then the younger brothers or their issue successively, according to seniority; and in default of such issue, then the sisters of the mother, to the total exclusion of all the relatives of the father. Now you will observe, that if the son of the mother who had thus bought lands had himself been the purchaser of the lands in question, and had died without issue, they would have descended, if he had been an only child, to the eldest brother of his father, or his heir *ex parte paternâ*, in the first instance, and on failure of all paternal heirs, then and then only to his heirs on the part of his mother. But, as the lands originally came from the mother, this rule provided that they should

Ex parte maternâ.

descend to the heir of the family from which the lands were originally derived.

So, in the case which we have put of *possessio fratris*, the eldest son, by gaining an actual seisin, himself became the stock of descent, and the lands descended to his heirs; but with this limitation, that such heirs were of the blood of his father, the purchaser. If, therefore, his father's relations should all have become extinct, his mother's relatives never could come in; for they were not of the father's blood. Whereas, had the son been himself the purchaser, his mother's relatives, being of his own blood, would have been entitled to come in as his heirs, in due course, after the failure of those of the blood of his father.

Breaking the descent.

A person entitled by descent from his mother or from any other ancestor might, if he pleased, so deal with the lands, which had descended to him, as to *break the descent*, as it was called, and to give himself a title to them, not as heir by descent, but as a purchaser. And in that case he would cause the lands to descend, on his decease intestate, not solely to his heir on the part of his mother or other ancestor, but first to his heir on the part of his father, according to the ordinary rule. Now in order to make himself the purchaser, it was necessary that he should part with the whole estate; and then take a re-conveyance of it back again to himself and his heirs. If he did this, the lands, on his decease, would descend to his heirs, he being the purchaser, and not to his heirs on the part of his mother or other ancestor, because he was no longer entitled to them by descent from the mother or other ancestor. In order to effect this change in the descendible quality of the land, it was necessary that there should be *two distinct conveyances* in fee: the first passing the lands to a third person; and the second then repassing them, from such third person, to the heir-at-law. For, if the heir simply made the conveyance to another person to the use of himself in fee, or to the use of a trustee upon trust for himself in fee, the beneficial interest would still descend in the same way as if he had made no such conveyance, namely, to his heir *ex parte maternâ*, or on the part of the ancestor from whom he inherited.

The act to amend the law of inheritance has, as we shall see, altered the law in this respect; but the learning with respect to breaking the descendible quality of an estate that has descended *ex parte maternâ* is still of use in respect to estates under the new law; as we shall hereafter see.

6th rule.

Half blood excluded.

The *6th rule* of descent was, that the collateral heir of the person last seised must be his next collateral kinsman of the whole blood. Under the old law any person related to him who was the stock of descent as half-brother or half-cousin was altogether excluded from the chance of inheriting. Thus, in the case of *possessio fratris* the seisin obtained by the elder brother was not only the means of enabling his sister of the whole blood to inherit before her half-brother; but it was also the means of totally excluding her half-brother from all hope of the inheritance. This now has been very properly altered, as we shall see.

7th rule.

The *7th rule* was that in collateral inheritance the male stock should be preferred to the female, that is, kindred derived from the male ancestors, however remote, should be admitted before those of the blood of the female ancestors, however near; unless where the lands had in fact descended from a female. When the lands have in fact descended from a female, as where they have descended to a man from his mother, there we have seen that his heir on the part of his mother will be entitled to inherit. But if this has not been the case,—if the man was himself a purchaser, or if he were entitled by descent from his father, or grandfather as the purchaser,—in that case the male stock were always preferred. In default of the issue of the person last seised, you sought the heir of his father, following, with regard to his father, the same rules as you had followed with regard to himself—viz., preferring the males to the females; taking the eldest of the males, when there were two or more in equal degree; taking the females altogether; and placing the lineal descendants, *in infinitum*, of any person deceased in the place of their ancestor. Subject to these rules, the first persons to inherit, in default of a man's issue, were the brothers and sisters of a man's father. In default of the brothers and sisters of the father, or their descendants in their place, you next sought the brothers of his grandfather in order, and then the sisters of the grandfather altogether, and so back again to the male paternal ancestors, as far as it was possible to reach. In default of the male paternal ancestors, came the female paternal ancestors and their descendants. And in default of all these, and only in default of all these, the relations of the mother came in.

Devise to heirs.

Under the old law, as under the present, the devisee under a will was a purchaser. But if a man seised in fee of lands devised them by his will to his heir at law, even though subject to debts or other incumbrances, or though in remainder expectant on the determination of any prior estate or estates, as for life or otherwise, yet the heir at law took by his prior title as heir by descent, and not by purchase under the will. If, however, the devisor altered the estate and limited it differently from what it would have descended to the heir, then the heir took by purchase, and became himself the stock of descent. Thus, if a person had several daughters and no son, and devised his lands to them in fee as joint tenants or as tenants in common, here they took by purchase. For had they succeeded as heirs they would have taken in coparcenary, which is a different method of holding lands from either joint tenancy or tenancy in common. So where a man, having two daughters (one of whom died leaving a son), devised his land to the son of his deceased daughter, the son was held to take as a purchaser. For by this devise there was an alteration of the estate; for if the land had descended, the devisee and the other daughter would have taken as coparceners. But when the devise was made of all to one, then the devisee took by purchase in a different manner from what would have been, had the land descended (*p*). But if lands were devised in fee to the heir, subject to an executory devise over to some other person on a given event, the heir would still have taken by descent, so long as his estate remained undefeated by the gift over.

Estate tail.

The descent of an estate tail under the old law was the same as it is now under the act to amend the law of inheritance. An estate tail was an estate limited to a man and the heirs of his body; and each heir of his body was said to claim *per formam doni*, according to the form of the gift; and he claimed as heir of the body of the first *donee* or *grantee* in tail. The consequence was, that the doctrine of *possessio fratris* did not apply to an estate tail, that is to say:—Suppose the tenant in tail died, leaving a son and a daughter by his first wife, and a son by his second wife. The son by the first wife is the heir of his body; this son now dies without having actually entered upon the property; and the heir of the body of his father is his half brother, who is also in fact the heir general of the father. But let the eldest son enter and take possession, and live for a

(*p*) *Reading* v. *Rawsterne*, 2 Ld. Raymond, 829.

number of years and then die; still the property goes *per formam doni*, not to the heir of his body, *as his heir*, but to the heir of the body of his father. And the heir of the body of his father is, if the elder son die without issue, the younger son by the second marriage. So that the fact that the elder son has taken possession made and still makes no difference whatever, in the descent of an estate tail. He could not constitute himself as the stock of descent, by any actual seisin on his part; for, by the terms of the gift, the inheritance was always to descend to the heirs of the body of his father. It is true that, on his decease leaving a son, the lands would descend to his son, who no doubt was the heir of his body. But it is not in that capacity that the son takes; the son takes as the then heir of the body of his grandfather. In all cases, therefore, of the descent of an estate tail, the stock of descent, that is, the person, the heir of whose body is to be sought for, is the original donee or grantee in tail. In this respect, as I have said, the law is the same now as it was before the passing of the act to amend the law of inheritance.

We have still to consider the descent under the old law of a remainder or reversion expectant on an estate of freehold. This must be reserved for my next Lecture.

LECTURE V.

In my last Lecture we considered the rules or canons of descent under the old law with respect to an estate in fee simple in possession, and also with respect to an estate tail. We now come to consider those rules with respect to a reversion or remainder expectant on an estate of freehold. A person might have settled land on A. for life, with remainder to B. in fee simple. A. then would, during the whole of his life, be the person actually seised. But B. might have died in the lifetime of A., leaving an heir; and that heir might himself have also died in the lifetime of A., leaving another heir, and the question then would be from whom the descent should be traced—whether the person to inherit should be the next heir of B., or whether he should be the next heir of the heir of B. who had just died. On this subject, Mr. Watkins, in his Treatise on the Law of Descent, writes as follows (*a*) :—

Descent of reversion or remainder on estate of freehold.

"If such hereditaments were leased or limited for life or in tail, so that an estate of freehold was created, then the seisin or possession in deed is in such particular tenant. And though a person is said to be seised of such reversion or remainder thus expectant upon an estate of freehold, and such seisin is often styled a seisin in law, and so a seisin in deed and a seisin in law be supposed to exist together of the same estate, yet this confusion seems to have arisen from the different acceptations in which the word *seisin* has been taken, and from using it in a general sense when it should be

(*a*) Page 35, 4th ed.

taken in a strict or confined one, or in a confined one when it should be used in a general sense."

"By the seisin of such reversioner or remainderman is meant, in reality, no more than that such reversioner continues, or that such remainderman is placed, in the tenancy, and that the property is fixed in him. The particular estates and the reversion or remainder over form in law but one estate, and consequently by delivering the possession to the person first taking, it extends to all. All, therefore, may be said to be seised, as they are all placed in the tenancy, and as the property is fixed in all. If the tenant for life surrender to him immediately in remainder, and the remainderman agree to such surrender, the frank-tenement is immediately in him; and a *præcipe quod reddat* lies against him before entry, but before entry he shall not have trespass. But on the other hand, when the seisin is divided into a seisin in deed and a seisin in law, we confine it merely to the present corporeal possession of the premises, not extending it to the fixture of an interest, which is to come into actual enjoyment on a future event. The seisin, not strictly in its technical sense, but in its primitive and vulgar acceptation, *i.e.*, the corporeal or visible possession, must, in the last case, be really expectant upon and postponed to the determination of the particular estate. And in this sense the reversioner or remainderman cannot be seised either in deed or in law."

As the seisin of the freehold is in A., who is called the particular tenant, or the tenant of the particular estate, and could not be in the heir of B. the remainderman, the consequence was, that, on the death of such heir, the reversion or remainder descended, not to his heir, but to the heir of B., the first purchaser. It was competent, however, for the first heir of B. to cause himself to become the stock of descent, by doing any act of ownership equivalent in the eye of the law to the obtaining actual seisin, had the estate been one in possession. A lease of the remainder or reversion for life or in tail, or a conveyance of it in fee to another person to his own use in fee, or to a trustee and his heirs in trust for himself and his heirs, were sufficient for this purpose (*b*). He then became the stock of descent, and on his decease intestate, the reversion or remainder descended to his own heir on the part of B., his ancestor, and not to the heir of B., his ancestor.

Equivalent to actual seisin.

We shall see that, under the act to amend the law of inheritance, land in possession now descends in the same manner as a reversion or remainder expectant in an estate of freehold descended under the old law. On the death of the ancestor the law cast the ancestor's reversion or remainder upon his heir. He could not enter because the tenant for life was in possession, but, being heir, he had the whole reversion or remainder vested in himself. This vested estate in reversion or remainder he was able to dispose of by deed or by will, if he thought fit to do so. But if he did not think fit to do so, then, on his decease, the reversion or remainder did not descend to his heir, because he was not the stock of descent, but it descended to the heir of B., the first purchaser. It was competent for him, however, either by the means we have mentioned, to make himself the stock of descent, or to do more, to make himself the purchaser. This he did by the same means by which the descent of an estate in fee simple was changed, viz. by alienating the reversion to some other person, and then taking it back again from that other person by purchase. In this case the reversion or remainder became descendible to his heirs generally and not merely to his heirs of the blood of the first purchaser.

Change of descent of reversion.

(*b*) Watkins on Descent, p. 115, 4th ed.

Stat. 3 & 4 Will. 4, c. 106.

We now come to consider the changes which were made by the Act to amend the Law of Inheritance, namely, the statute 3 & 4 Will. IV. c. 106. This act came into operation on the 1st of January, 1834; and it does not extend to any descent which took place on the death of any person who died before that date. The act provides (*c*) that where any assurance executed before the first of January, 1834, or the will of any person who died before that day, shall have contained any limitation or gift to the heir or heirs of any person, under which the person or persons answering the description of heir shall be entitled to an estate by purchase, then the person or persons, who would have answered such description of heir if the act had not been made, shall become entitled by virtue of such limitation or gift, whether the person named as ancestor shall or shall not have been living on or after the 1st of January, 1834. This was quite right. The act amended the law of inheritance. But it was not intended to deprive any person, to whom a gift had been made in his capacity of heir, of the benefit intended for him, or to give it to some other person than the one whom the donor intended. The act extends to all hereditaments, whether corporeal or incorporeal, and whether freehold or copyhold, or of any other tenure, and whether descendible according to the common law, or according to the custom of gavelkind or borough English, or any other custom, and in fact to every interest that is capable of being inherited.

The purchaser.

The most important enactment in the act is that contained in the former part of the 2nd section, viz. that *in every case descent shall be traced from the purchaser*. The purchaser is defined to be the person who last acquired the land otherwise than by descent, or than by any escheat, partition or inclosure, by the effect of which

(*c*) Sect. 12.

the land shall have become part of or descendible in the same manner as other land acquired by descent. This explanation requires itself to be explained. If a person acquires land by descent, it is sufficiently obvious that he is not the purchaser. But if he claims under a voluntary deed or under a will he is as much a purchaser in the eye of the law as if he had bought the property for money. Now the lord of a manor may, as we have seen (*d*), acquire land by *escheat;* and he may acquire it, either in the case of a freehold tenant or in the case of a copyhold tenant; and the effect of escheat is somewhat different in each case. If a freehold tenant dies without heirs, the lord of the manor, of whom he held, becomes entitled to his tenements by escheat. The land becomes re-united to the manor, and again forms part thereof, and becomes descendible in the same way that the manor previously descended. In the case of escheat of copyholds, the lord, who was before seised in fee of the copyhold land, remains seised in fee of it still; and all that is done is, that the land, which was his before, subject to a tenancy at will, which by custom practically deprived him of the holding of the land, now becomes his for his own benefit, discharged from any such tenancy. The difference between freehold and copyhold tenure is well illustrated in the case of a re-purchase by the lord of the land of one of his tenants. If the lord of a manor purchase of one of his freehold tenants the freehold tenement which the tenant previously held, the lord no doubt is entitled to the lands he has bought; but they no longer form part of the manor, and would not pass by a conveyance of the manor, or by a devise of the manor in a will made anterior to the purchase. But if the lord of a manor should purchase the copyhold lands of one of his tenants, the lands will again form part of the manor, in the same way as if the lord had gained them by

Escheat.

Re-purchase.

(*d*) *Ante*, pp. 20, 34.

escheat; and they will pass by a conveyance or devise of the manor. For in truth the lands all along have been in law the lands of the lord and part of his manor; and, by the purchase of the copyhold interest, they simply become discharged from a burdensome tenancy, which by custom was previously attached to them. You will find the law on this subject laid down in the case of *Delacherois* v. *Delacherois*, which is a case in the House of Lords, reported in the 11th volume of the House of Lords Reports, p. 62. The judgment of Lord St. Leonards in that case (p. 98), is particularly worthy of attention.

Delacherois v. *Delacherois*.

Partition.

But a purchaser is a person who has acquired his land otherwise than by *partition*, by the effect of which the land shall have become part of, or descendible in the same manner as, other land acquired by descent. If co-heirs, who, you will remember, are called in law coparceners, and who become entitled by descent in equal shares, should make *partition* between themselves of the land descended, allotting one part in *severalty* to one, and another part in *severalty* to another, the law was anciently, and is still, that the part so allotted by partition to each coparcener descends in the same way as the undivided share of the land to which such coparcener was entitled previously to partition (*e*).

Inclosure.

Again, the purchaser is a person who has acquired the land otherwise than by any inclosure, by the effect of which the land shall have become part of, or descendible in the same manner as, other land acquired by descent. Inclosure here means inclosure by virtue of the powers of some inclosure act. In the first instance inclosure acts each contained several provisions; and in the early acts the provisions were often obscure and inadequate. A general inclosure act, embodying many

(*e*) *Doe* d. *Crosthwaite* v. *Dixon*, 5 Ad. & Ell. 834.

of the provisions usually inserted in acts for the inclosure of commons, was passed in the forty-first year of the reign of King George III. (*f*). This act provided (*g*) for partition between joint tenants, coparceners or tenants in common, and for allotment to such owners or proprietors in severalty, which allotments were to be holden in the same manner as the undivided shares of such estates would have been held, in case such partition and division had not been made. And in every inclosure act there was a provision to the effect that the allotments, under the inclosure act, should have in every respect the same title as the interests in respect of which they were made. If, therefore, any interest in the common inclosed was acquired by descent, the allotment in respect of it was treated as having been acquired in the same way. In the reign of her present majesty another *general act* was passed to facilitate the inclosure and improvement of commons and land held in common and for other purposes. This act is statute 8 & 9 of the Queen, c. 118, and it provides (*h*), "That all such land as shall be taken in exchange or on partition, or be allotted by virtue of that act, shall be held by the person to whom it shall be given in exchange or on partition, or allotted, under the same tenures, rents, customs and services as the land, in respect of which such land shall have been given in exchange or on partition, or allotted, would have been held, in case no such exchange, partition or inclosure had been made. And the land taken in exchange, or on partition, or allotted in respect of freehold, shall be deemed freehold; and the land taken in exchange or on partition, or allotted in respect of copyhold or customary land, shall be deemed copyhold or customary land, and shall be held of the lord of the same manor, under the same rent, and by the same customs and services as the copy-

Stat. 8 & 9 Vict. c. 118, s. 94.

(*f*) Stat. 41 Geo. III. c. 109.
(*g*) Sect. 16.
(*h*) Sect. 94.

hold or customary land in respect of which it may have been taken in exchange or on partition, or allotted, was or ought to have been held, and shall pass in like manner as the copyhold or customary land in respect whereof such exchanges, partitions or allotments shall be made; and as to copyhold and customary allotments, without any new admittance in respect of the land taken or allotted respectively." You see, therefore, that in the special cases of escheat, partition or inclosure, land which may not actually have been acquired by inheritance is considered as having been acquired in that way, whenever it becomes descendible in the same manner as other land acquired by descent.

Descent.

The second section of the act to amend the law of inheritance provides that in every case *descent* shall be traced from the purchaser. The word *descent* is defined to mean the title to inherit land by reason of consanguinity, as well where the heir shall be an ancestor or collateral relation as where he shall be a child or other issue, and the expression *descendants* of any ancestor shall extend to all persons who must trace their descent through such ancestor. You will see that land now, sometimes, not only descends but ascends, that is, goes back to the father or other lineal ancestor of the person from whom the descent is to be traced. The second section goes on with a provision which, perhaps, I had better notice before descanting further on the former part of this section, and that is this: "To the intent that the pedigree may never be carried further back than the circumstances of the case and the nature of the title shall require, the person *last entitled to the land* shall, for the purposes of this act, be considered to have been the purchaser thereof, unless it shall be proved that he inherited the same, in which case the person from whom he inherited the same shall be considered to have been the purchaser, unless it shall be proved that he inherited the same; and, in like manner, the last person from whom the land shall be proved to have been inherited shall in every case be considered to have been the purchaser, unless it shall be proved that he inherited the same." The person last entitled is defined to be the last person who had a right to the land, whether he did or did not obtain the possession or receipt of the rents or profits thereof. I myself never could see any particular advantage in this provision. It seems to provide that if you cannot prove that a person inherited, you must then take it for granted that he acquired his land by purchase. Perhaps it was as well expressly to enact that such should be the case; but, in the absence of any such provision, it seems to me that if you have a person entitled to lands and do not know how he came by them, the presumption would be that he was the purchaser; at any rate you would have to seek, on his death intestate, for his heir, and not for the heir of any other person, because it would be impossible to know what other person's heir you should seek for.

Person last entitled.

In the case, therefore, which we have put of *possessio fratris*, viz., of the case of a man dying intestate, leaving a son and a daughter by his former wife, and a son by his second wife, you will see that the law is materially altered by the act to amend the law of inheritance. The eldest son, whether he enter or not, is to be deemed the purchaser, unless it be proved that he inherited; but, if it be proved that he inherited, then he is not the purchaser, whether he has or has not acquired seisin of the land, and so cannot be the stock of descent. Under the old law, the question was—has he, or has he not, obtained an actual seisin? If he had obtained actual seisin, then the lands descended to his heir, in this case his sister of the whole blood. If he had not obtained actual seisin, then the lands descended to his younger

No *possessio fratris* under present law.

brother of the half blood, as being the next heir of his father, who was the person last actually seised. Now, when you have found the purchaser, the descent in every case must be traced from him; that is to say, you must look for *his* heir, however long ago he may have died. When, therefore, the eldest son in this case dies intestate (if he should die so), the lands will not, as is popularly supposed, descend to his heir, but they will descend to the heir of his father, the last purchaser, however long ago he may have died. The old rule of *possessio fratris* is abolished. No person actually entitled by inheritance can be now the stock of descent, unless he is looked upon by law as a purchaser, in consequence of there being no proof that he actually took by inheritance. There is one exception to this rule engrafted on the act by a subsequent enactment, as we shall hereafter see.

Descent traced from purchaser.

The descent of an estate in possession is therefore now similar to the descent of an estate in reversion or remainder expectant upon an estate of freehold, under the old law. Under that law, the seisin being in the tenant for life, the heir of the reversioner or remainderman could not obtain seisin; and so, though he had a vested interest, which he could dispose of by deed or will, yet on his death intestate the reversion or remainder descended to the heir of the first purchaser of the reversion or remainder, and not to the heir of such heir.

The first canon of descent is therefore altered. Hereditaments no longer lineally descend to the issue of the person *who was last seised, in infinitum;* but they lineally descend *in infinitum* to the issue of *the last purchaser.*

The first canon is also materially altered in its second branch, viz. thus: That lands shall never lineally ascend. Under the present act they do, in some cases, lineally ascend, for the act enacts (*i*), that every lineal ancestor shall be capable of being heir to any of his issue; and in every case where there shall be no issue of the purchaser, his nearest lineal ancestor shall be his heir, in preference to any person who would have been entitled to inherit, either by tracing his descent through such lineal ancestor, or in consequence of there being no descendant of such lineal ancestor; so that the father shall be preferred to a brother or sister, and a more remote lineal ancestor to any of his issue, other than a nearer lineal ancestor or his issue.

Lineal ancestor.

Thus, if a person purchases land, and dies possessed thereof intestate and without issue, his father, if living, will be his heir-at-law.

Next to the father, however, come the father's issue, as representing him by the 4th canon, which still remains in force, and is applicable to the law as it exists under the present act, viz. this: That the lineal descendants *in infinitum* of any person deceased shall represent their ancestor. Under the old law, you will remember, a father could not inherit (*j*), and the brother of the person who was the stock of descent was considered, in case of the death of that person without issue, to inherit immediately from him as his next heir. But the present act now provides (*k*), that no brother or sister shall be considered to inherit immediately from his or her brother or sister, but every descent from a brother or sister shall be traced through the parent.

Descent from brother now traced through parent.

Suppose that there be no issue of the purchaser, nor of his father, and at his decease his father is dead, but his father's father is living, then his father's father shall be his heir-at-law. For the male line is strictly preferred, and all the male paternal ancestors

Paternal grandfather.

(*i*) Sect. 6. (*j*) *Ante*, p. 58. (*k*) Sect. 5.

in upward succession, one after another, and their issue in their places, precede those who claim on the female side. The course of descent in this respect is marked out by the 7th section of the act, which provides, that none of the maternal ancestors of the person from whom the descent is to be traced, nor any of their descendants, shall be capable of inheriting, until all his paternal ancestors and their descendants shall have failed; and also that no female paternal ancestor of such person, nor any of her descendants, shall be capable of inheriting until all his male paternal ancestors and their descendants shall have failed; and that no female maternal ancestor of such person, nor any of her descendants, shall be capable of inheriting until all his male maternal ancestors and their descendants shall have failed (*l*).

Males preferred.

There is another provision in the act which provides for an event of very rare occurrence, but which was in former times the subject of much controversy, and was one of the few points in which the law of inheritance was uncertain, and that is this—whether, when you have exhausted all the male paternal ancestors and their descendants, and can go back no further into antiquity in search of such descendants, you should seek for the mother of the *most remote* male paternal ancestor that you can find, or the mother of the nearest male paternal ancestor, namely, the mother of the father of the purchaser. The act settles the question in favour of the mother of the *most remote* rather than the less remote paternal ancestor. And also, in the same manner, when the paternal ancestors have failed, the mother of the more remote male *maternal* ancestor is preferred to the

Mother of most remote ancestor preferred.

(*l*) The case of *Greaves* v. *Greenwood*, L. R., 2 Ex. Div. 289, decided since these lectures were delivered, is an interesting case on the amount of evidence which is necessary to prove the failure of any given line of ancestors.

mother of any less remote. The 8th section enacts, that where there shall be a failure of male paternal ancestors of the person from whom the descent is to be traced, and their descendants, the mother of his more remote male paternal ancestor, or her descendants, shall be the heir or heirs of such person in preference to the mother of a less remote male paternal ancestor or her descendants; and where there shall be a failure of male maternal ancestors of such person and their descendants, the mother of his more remote male maternal ancestor, and her descendants, shall be the heir or heirs of such person in preference to the mother of a less remote male maternal ancestor and her descendants.

Lineal descendants represent their ancestor.

The 4th canon—that all the lineal descendants *in infinitum* shall represent their ancestor—is still law. Thus, suppose a person to purchase land, and to die intestate, leaving a daughter and the only son of another daughter, who has died in his lifetime. The heirs of the purchaser will be the surviving daughter and the only son of the deceased daughter, who will take in equal shares, the son of the deceased daughter representing his parent. But suppose that this should happen, that the father should die intestate leaving two daughters, and that afterwards one of the daughters should die intestate leaving an only son. The question arises, to whom will her share descend? It has been argued that as, under the act, descent is to be traced from the purchaser, and as the heir of the purchaser is the other daughter and the son of the deceased daughter in equal shares, therefore the moiety which belonged to the deceased daughter by descent from her father would on her death go, one half to her sister and the other half to her son. This, however, is not the law. The rule of representation still takes place, and was not intended to be affected by the statute. And the son of the daughter lately deceased will take the whole of his mother's share by representation from her. You will find an argument of mine on this subject in Appendix B. to my Principles of the Law of Real Property (*m*). The point is now established by authority, having been decided by the late Vice-Chancellor Shadwell in the case of *Cooper* v. *France* (*n*); and, on the authority of this case, a decision to the same effect was made by the Court of Common Pleas in the case of *Lewin* v. *Lewin*, in which I was counsel, on 21st November, 1874; but as this is an important decision, and one that has never been reported, I propose to give you an account of it. With this case I hope to commence my next Lecture, which I hope will bring us to the end of that part of our subject which relates to the seisin of the freehold as it affects descent.

Cooper v. *France.*

Lewin v. *Lewin.*

(*m*) Page 475, 12th ed.

(*n*) 14 Jur. 214; 19 L. J., N. S., Chanc. 313.

LECTURE VI.

In my last Lecture I promised to give you an account of the case of *Lewin* v. *Lewin*, as a striking illustration of the rule that the issue of a person always represent their ancestor, and stand in his place. The plaintiff, William Henry Lewin, sued his uncle, Frederick Mortimer Lewin, the defendant, for a sum of money, claimed by the plaintiff as his share of the rents of an estate known as the Hollies Estate, in the county of Kent, and also in respect of the defendant having committed waste in cutting down timber on the estate; and by consent of the parties, and by the order of Mr. Justice Denman, dated the 25th of November, 1873, according to the Common Law Procedure Act, 1852, the case was stated without pleadings for the opinion of the court. It appeared that by indentures of lease and release, dated the 4th and 5th of July, 1810, the Hollies Estate in the parish of Bexley, in the county of Kent, was conveyed to Thomas Lewin in fee simple as purchaser thereof. The custom of gavelkind in the county of Kent applied to all the lands mentioned in the case. Thomas Lewin died on the 17th of September, 1854, intestate and without having ever been married. Thomas Lewin had four brothers and no more, namely, the defendant Frederick Mortimer Lewin and three other brothers, one of whom, William Charles James Lewin, was the father of the plaintiff. The plaintiff's father died in the lifetime of Thomas Lewin, leaving four sons and no more him surviving; one of whom was the plaintiff William Henry Lewin, and another was Octavius Hippesley Lewin, with regard to whose share in the lands the

Lewin v. *Lewin.*

question arose. All the above four sons of the deceased brother were living at the time of the death of Thomas Lewin. On the death of Thomas Lewin the Hollies Estate, therefore, descended, according to the custom of gavelkind, to his three surviving brothers, and to the sons of his deceased brother, in the following shares, (that is to say,) one undivided fourth part of the estate to each of his three surviving brothers; and the remaining undivided fourth part descended in equal undivided fourth parts, one to each of the aforesaid four sons of his deceased brother, being nephews of the said Thomas Lewin. Then, by an order of partition made by the Enclosure Commissioners for England and Wales on the 20th November, 1872, certain lands and hereditaments, being part of the said Hollies Estate, were allotted in severalty to the defendant, in respect of his one-fourth part or share of the said estate. The residue of the said estate was also thereby allotted in severalty to the other parties entitled thereto, but was not partitioned or divided between them. The effect of this order was, as we have seen (*a*), not to make any of the parties purchasers in respect of the lands allotted to them. The allotted land descended in exactly the same manner as the undivided shares in the whole estate would have descended, had no such partition been made. And the effect was simply this, to alter the fractions; so that, whereas the four sons of the deceased brother were, before the partition, each entitled to one-fourth of one-fourth or one-sixteenth of the whole estate; after the partition they became each entitled to one-fourth of one-third, or one-twelfth, of that part of the estate which had been allotted to the two other surviving brothers and the sons of the third brother between them. The defendant acquired at different times from the different co-heirs by far the largest portion of the allotted estate; and he was, by himself or his tenants, in possession of the

(*a*) Ante, p. 72.

whole of the estate, and in receipt of the rents and profits thereof; and he cut down timber belonging to the freehold and inheritance of the estate. One of the plaintiff's brothers only, namely, Frederick Dealtry Lewin, was still living. Edward Powney Lewin, another brother, was killed at the siege of Lucknow in 1857. He had one child only, namely, a daughter, Ada Henrietta Lewin, who was still living. Octavius Hippesley Lewin, another of the plaintiff's brothers, died on the 24th August, 1871, intestate, without having ever been married, and the question was, to whom did his share of the allotted estate descend? It was contended on behalf of the defendant that the descent was to be traced from Thomas Lewin, the purchaser, over again; and that as the defendant Frederick Mortimer Lewin was confessedly one of the co-heirs of Thomas Lewin, his brother, he ought to have a share in the share of which Octavius Hippesley Lewin, his nephew, died seised. But it was held by the court that the rule of representation prevailed; and that, although the descent was to be traced from Thomas Lewin as the last purchaser, yet, so long as any issue of the deceased brother remained, the share which such deceased brother would have inherited as co-heir to the intestate, had he survived him, could not go beyond his own issue. It was held therefore that the share of Octavius Hippesley descended to the following persons as the co-heirs of Thomas Lewin, quoad that share, namely, one-third to the plaintiff, one-third to Frederick Dealtry Lewin, and the other one-third to Ada Henrietta Lewin, as the only child and heiress of her father, Edward Powney Lewin. You see that the question as to the share of the rents and the share of the timber decided the question as to the share of the lands. The counsel in the case were myself, Mr. Philbrick, Q. C., and Mr. R. E. Webster, on behalf of the plaintiff, and Mr. Manisty, Q. C., and another gentleman whose name I forget, on behalf of the defendant. The court was composed of Mr. Justice Brett and Mr. Justice Keating, sitting in Banco.

5th rule, how altered.

The fifth canon under the old law was, that on failure of lineal descendants or issue, the inheritance should descend to collateral relations of the person last seised, *being of the blood of the first purchaser*, subject to the three preceding rules. Now, as you see, on failure of lineal descendants or issue of the purchaser, the inheritance descends to his lineal ancestors, and if they are dead, then to his collateral relations, only as representing their deceased ancestors; and such collateral relations must of course be of his blood. The purchaser now is the person in all cases whose heir is to be sought; and if his lineal descendants fail, you seek for his ancestors or their issue. And it must always be carefully borne in mind that it is the *purchaser* whose heir is to be sought for, and not the heir of the person last seised of the land; unless that person was himself a purchaser, or unless it cannot be proved that he took by inheritance. An heir, no doubt, may make himself a purchaser; and every conveyance and re-conveyance which, under the old law, was sufficient to change the course of descent in the case of a person entitled *ex parte maternâ* (*b*), is sufficient under the law, as it now exists, to make the heir a purchaser. But the act to amend the law of inheritance goes further, and provides (*c*), that when any land shall have been limited by any assurance, executed after the 31st of December, 1833, to the person or to the heirs of the person who shall thereby have conveyed the same land, such person shall be considered to have acquired the same as a purchaser by virtue of such assurance, and shall not be considered as entitled thereto as of his former estate or part thereof. The word "land" extends, in the construction of the act, to every interest capable of being inherited. If,

How an heir may make himself a purchaser.

(*b*) Ante, p. 62. (*c*) Sect. 3.

therefore, a person entitled as heir should now convey the land to another person in fee, to the use of himself (*d*), or unto and to the use of a trustee, upon trust for himself, he would, by means of the section we have just quoted, become the purchaser within the meaning of the act. The interest thus created would be land limited to the person who shall thereby have conveyed the same land; and such interest would, on his decease intestate, go to his heir, and not to the heir of the person from whom he inherited.

No descent now to heir *ex parte maternâ*.

You thus see that, under the present law, there is no such thing as a descent of land to the heir of A. B. *ex parte maternâ* or *ex parte paternâ*. Under the old law, the heir to lands which had descended from a mother, was the heir, *ex parte maternâ*, *of the person last seised*. Now the heir to such lands is the heir *of the mother*—the last purchaser. So great, however, is the influence of old ideas and phrases, that you still continually hear lawyers talking of descent to an heir *ex parte maternâ* or *ex parte paternâ*, just as if the law on this point had never been altered.

Nanson v. *Barnes*.

The case of *Nanson* v. *Barnes* (*e*) is a good illustration of the doctrine respecting the breaking of the descent of lands which have descended from an ancestor on the mother's side. The case was this: One George Blamire, who died in September, 1863, was entitled, by descent from his mother, as her only son and heir-at-law, to certain lands which are said to have been customary freeholds. The evidence showed that the testator's mother was, at a court holden for the manor of which the lands were parcel, on the 19th of October, 1815, admitted tenant to those lands as the

(*d*) Per Shadwell, V.-C., in *Strickland* v. *Strickland*, 10 Sim. 375, 376; per Lord Romilly, M. R., in *Heywood* v. *Heywood*, 34 Beav. 322.

(*e*) L. R., 7 Eq. 250.

only daughter and customary heiress of Thomas Harrington; and that on the 2nd of May, 1832, which was before the act to amend the law of inheritance took effect, the testator was admitted tenant as only son and heir-at-law of his mother. On the same day George Blamire conveyed these lands to William Nanson in fee, according to the custom of the manor, by surrender and admittance; and, by a deed of even date, William Nanson declared that he and his heirs should be seised of the lands, upon trust for such persons as George Blamire by any deed or by his last will should appoint, and in default thereof in trust for George Blamire, his heirs and assigns for ever, according to the custom of the manor. George Blamire then made a will, by which he gave all his real estates to Sir James Graham, Bart., absolutely. But Sir James Graham having died in his lifetime, the devise contained in the will lapsed. The lands therefore descended to the heir of the purchaser; and the real question was, whether George Blamire, by the conveyance and declaration of trust above mentioned, had made himself a purchaser; or, whether the lands were to descend to the next heir of Thomas Harrington, his maternal grandfather, from whom the lands had descended to him. I say the real question; for you will find that, oddly enough, the chief clerk in his certificate, the counsel in their arguments, the court in its judgment, and the reporter in his head-note, all treat the case as a question between the *heirs of George Blamire ex parte maternâ*, and *his* heirs *ex parte paternâ*. Now, as you know, George Blamire was the stock of descent, only in case he was a purchaser. If he was still entitled by descent, the lands went, on his decease, not to *his* heir *ex parte maternâ*, but to the heir of his maternal grandfather—the first purchaser. Two ladies were found, by the chief clerk's certificate, to be the co-heiresses of George Blamire on the part of his father; and a Mr. Langley was found to be his heir on the part of his mother. It should have been said that the two ladies were his co-heiresses-at-law; and that Mr. Langley was the heir-at-law of Thomas Harrington, his maternal grandfather. The court held, that the conveyance of the 2nd of May, 1832, did not make George Blamire a purchaser. His Honor was of opinion that, so far from divesting himself of his whole estate, and taking back a new one, it was perfectly clear that, taking the two deeds together, as they must be taken, for it was one transaction, the operation of them was merely to give him a more complete dominion over it. By the first deed the trustee took the estate absolutely, but he had no beneficial ownership; and, by the second deed, the real owner obtained a larger dominion over the property, which consisted in a power to devise it, a dominion which he had not before. "In my opinion," said his Honor, "the testator did not take back a new estate by purchase. These deeds were part of one transaction for a recognized purpose. The chief clerk has certified rightly in favour of the heir *ex parte maternâ*." This certificate, no doubt, was substantially right; but it should properly have been in favour of Mr. Langley, *as the heir of Thomas Harrington*, the last purchaser, and not as the heir of George Blamire *ex parte maternâ*. Had the deed in question been executed after the 31st of December, 1833, then, under the 3rd section of the act, George Blamire would have been constituted a purchaser in respect of the equitable estate limited to him, and his co-heiresses-at-law would have been entitled; or if William Nanson, his trustee, had immediately resurrendered the lands to him, and he had been admitted, then he would have taken a new estate by purchase, and the lands would have descended to his co-heiresses-at-law.

The sixth canon of inheritance was, that the collateral heir of the person last seised must be his next collateral

Half blood.

kinsman of the whole blood. The half blood could never inherit. The most remote relations on the father's side were admitted as a man's heirs in preference to his half brother, who, whether on the part of his father, or on the part of his mother, was totally excluded. This was undoubtedly a great hardship; and it was remedied by the act to amend the law of inheritance. In its 9th section it is provided, "that any person related to the person from whom the descent is to be traced by the half blood, shall be capable of being his heir; and the place in which any such relation by the half blood shall stand in the order of inheritance, so as to be entitled to inherit, shall be next after any relation in the same degree of the whole blood and his issue, where the common ancestor shall be a male, and next after the common ancestor, where such common ancestor shall be a female. So that the brother of the half blood on the part of the father shall inherit next after the sisters of the whole blood on the part of the father and their issue; and the brother of the half blood on the part of the mother shall inherit next after the mother."

Thus, put the case we have before put of a man having a son and a daughter by his first wife, and a son by his second wife. If the father is the purchaser, the lands now descend first to the eldest son, next to the younger son, and next, if they both die without issue, to the daughter. Each child is of the whole blood to the parent of such child. But suppose, now, that the eldest son should be the purchaser, and should die intestate, and without issue, the lands will now descend, in the first place, to his father if he be living. If he be dead, they will descend to his sister as being of the whole blood, and who, though a female, is preferred to her half brother, because she is of the whole blood and he is of the half blood. This was the case before the act; but before the act the half brother could never come in; now he comes in next after the sister of the purchaser and her issue, should she have any to represent her. Under the 9th section of the act he has a title to inherit, and his title is next after his half sister, who is a relation in the same degree of the whole blood, and her issue.

If the whole of the paternal ancestors and their issue shall have been exhausted or shall have failed, the mother of the purchaser will be his heir; and, the half blood being now admitted, if she shall have had a child of the half blood to the purchaser, that child would, under the same section, now be the purchaser's heir-at-law, in preference to the father of the mother or any of his issue, and of course in preference to her grandfather, great grandfather, or any other more remote ancestor, or any of their descendants.

9th rule. Male stock preferred.

The ninth canon of inheritance is still the same, as in fact we have already seen, viz., that in collateral inheritance the male stock shall be preferred to the female: that is, kindred derived from the blood of the male ancestor, however remote, shall be admitted before those from the blood of the female, however near. The old canon, however, adds, "unless where the lands have in fact descended from a female." But if the lands have in fact descended from a female, however long ago that female may have died, now, as you have seen, the land descends, not to the heir of the last person seised, nor to the heir of the last person entitled, but to the heir of that female, she being the last purchaser. If, however, she were not the purchaser, but were herself entitled by descent, then you must go back to the heir of the purchaser. And if the purchaser died a century ago, or more than that, still, if there has been nothing but descent ever since, the law now is, that the stock of descent is the purchaser, and the land will always descend to the next heir of that purchaser, and not to the next heir of the person who was last seised or entitled.

Devise to heir.

You may remember that, under the old law, when a tenant in fee simple devised land to his heir-at-law, the heir was entitled by his prior title of inheritance, and was not considered to take as a devisee (*f*). This rule, however, has been altered by the act to amend the law of inheritance, which enacts (*g*) that, when any land shall have been devised by any testator, who shall die after the 31st day of December, 1833, to the heir, or to the person who shall be the heir, of such testator, such heir shall be considered to have acquired the land as a devisee, and not by descent. He will thenceforth become the purchaser from whom the descent is to be traced. It was also a rule under the old law that, when a person conveyed land by any deed in favour of others for life or in tail, with an ultimate reversion to himself and his heirs, or to his own right heirs, the ultimate reversion was merely part of his old estate, and descended in the same way as the estate would have done, if he had made no such conveyance (*h*). But in this respect also the act to amend the law of inheritance made a change, for it enacts, as we have seen (*i*), in the latter part of the 3rd section, that when any land shall have been limited by any assurance executed after the 31st day of December, 1833, to the person or to the heirs of the person who shall thereby have conveyed the same land, such person shall be considered to have acquired the same as a purchaser, by virtue of such assurance, and shall not be considered entitled thereto as of his former estate or part thereof.

I hardly know what was the object of this enactment,

(*f*) Ante, p. 64.

(*g*) Sect. 3.

(*h*) Ante, p. 63.

(*i*) Ante, p. 84.

unless it were to prevent the tracing of descent from remote purchasers, and, as far as possible, to make the last person entitled the stock of descent, by providing that he should be considered as a purchaser in cases where before he would not have been so.

However, the next enactment makes land now to descend from a distant ancestor, in cases where, before the act, it would have descended to the heirs of the person last seised.

This enactment, which is section 4, provides "that when any person shall have acquired any land *by purchase* under a limitation to the heirs, or to the heirs of the body of any of his ancestors, contained in an assurance executed after the 31st December, 1833, or under a limitation to the heirs or to the heirs of the body of any of his ancestors, or under any limitation having the same effect, contained in a will of any testator who shall depart this life after the 31st day of December, 1833, then and in any of such cases such land shall descend, and the descent thereof shall be traced as if the ancestor named in such limitation had been the purchaser of such land." Under the old law, as you may remember, when a purchaser died, the lands always descended to his heir, and not to the heir of anyone else; but it is now provided, that when a person becomes a *purchaser* under a limitation to the heirs or to the heirs of the body of any of his ancestors, or under any limitation having the same effect, contained in any assurances executed, or in a will of the testator dying, after the time when the act took effect, that the descent shall be traced as if the ancestor named in the limitation had been in fact the purchaser of the land; or as if the heir, who really claims by purchase, had in truth claimed by descent.

Sect. 4.
Limitation to heirs by purchase.

Under the old law, the fact that a man had been

Attainder.

sentenced to death for *treason or murder* was called *attainder*, and had the effect of corrupting his blood, as it was said, so that no person could trace descent either from him or through him, from any collateral relation. This hardship was remedied by the 10th section of the act, which provided, "that when any person, from whom the descent of any land is to be traced, shall have any relation, who, having been attainted, shall have died before such descent shall have taken place, then such attainder shall not prevent any person from inheriting such land, who would have been capable of inheriting the same, by tracing his descent through such relation, if he had not been attainted; unless such land shall have escheated in consequence of such attainder before the 1st day of January, 1834," when the act came into operation. I mentioned, however, in a former Lecture (*k*), that all escheats by reason of any *attainder*, and all attainders, are now swept away by the statute of 33 & 34 of the Queen, chap. 23, sect. 1.

Stat. 22 & 23 Vict. c. 35.

Descent to heirs of person last entitled.

The act to amend the law of inheritance has been amended by the statute of 22 & 23 of the Queen, chap. 35, which provides (*l*) that where there shall be a total failure of heirs of the purchaser, or where any land shall be descendible as if an ancestor had been the purchaser thereof (*m*), and there shall be a total failure of the heirs of such ancestor, then and in every such case the land shall descend, and the descent shall thenceforth be traced, from the person last entitled to the land, as if he had been the purchaser thereof. This section provides for such a case as the following:—Land has descended from A., the purchaser, to his eldest son as his heir-at-law; the eldest son dies intestate, and the lands descend to the heirs of his father. Before this enactment, they could not, on failure of his father's

(*k*) Ante, p. 33.

(*l*) Sect. 19.

(*m*) Sect. 4; ante, p. 91.

relations, have descended to the heirs of his mother; but, by this enactment, where there is a total failure of the heirs of his father, the purchaser, the lands shall descend as if the person last entitled had been the purchaser thereof. This enactment, therefore, has the effect, in the present instance, of letting in the mother and the mother's relations to succeed as heirs, if all the father's relations should have failed. This enactment was a tardy compliance with the recommendation of the Real Property Commissioners of 1833, who, in their first Report (n), recommended as follows:—"We further think that the last proprietor may be treated as if he had been first purchaser, in the rare case in which the line, from which the estate descended to the last proprietor, has failed, for the purpose of admitting to the inheritance his other relations, rather than let it escheat."

You will find in the chapter on descent in my "Principles of the Law of Real Property" (o), a table of descent under the act to amend the law of inheritance.

Gavelkind and borough English.

The customs of *gavelkind* and *borough English* are known to the law; and if any land, whether freehold or copyhold, is stated to be subject to either of these customs, then every right, estate or interest of any kind, which is descendible, will follow the custom, and go, in the case of gavelkind, to all the males equally, and, in the case of borough English, to the youngest of the sons (p). But if there should be in any manor a special custom of descent, not strictly according either to that of gavelkind or that of borough English, the custom is construed strictly; that is to say, the ordi-

Special custom construed strictly.

(n) Page 15.

(o) Page 111, 12th ed.

(p) *Baxter* v. *Dowdswell*, 2 Lev. 138.

nary course of the common law is not interfered with, except so far as the custom plainly varies it. Thus, if the custom be that all the customary *lands* have descended and ought to descend to the youngest son, youngest brother or youngest nephew, as the case may be, then, although lands will so descend, yet a *right* to the lands, which is not the same thing as the land itself, will not so descend, but will descend according to the course of the common law.

Rider v. *Wood.* The case of *Rider* v. *Wood* (*q*) illustrates both of these propositions.

In that case there was a devise by will to one William Goffe for life, with remainder to his eldest son in fee; with a further devise to the daughters of William Goffe as tenants in common, and their respective legal and customary heirs for ever, in the event of William Goffe leaving no son or issue of a son living at his death. This devise created, during the lifetime of William Goffe, what is called a contingent remainder to the daughters. There were two manors: in one of them descent was according to the custom of borough English simply; in the other manor the custom was stated to be "that the descent was to the youngest son or daughter or sister of the copyholder last seised." One of the daughters died in the lifetime of her father William Goffe, the tenant for life, without issue. It was held that her share in the property held of that manor, in which the descent was according to the custom of borough English, descended to her youngest sister then living, according to the custom of borough English; and that, on the subsequent birth of another sister, her share shifted to the subsequently born sister, as being the youngest. But, with regard to her share in that part of the property which was held of the manor, in which the custom

(*q*) 1 Kay & J. 644.

simply was, that descent was to the youngest son or daughter or sister of the copyholder last seised, the custom was strictly construed. The daughter in question, strictly speaking, was not seised. The seisin, although a *quasi* or *customary* seisin, was not in the daughter, but in her father, the tenant for life, and she had no estate in the premises. For a contingent remainder is not an estate, but a mere chance of having one; and a mere chance of having an estate is not a thing of which a person can, strictly speaking, be said to have even a *quasi* seisin. It was held, therefore, that in this manor, on the death of the daughter who died without issue, her interest, such as it was, descended, not according to the custom, but to all her sisters as her co-heiresses, according to the course of the common law.

There is another case with regard to customary descent; decided, first, by the Court of Exchequer, and afterwards on appeal by the Court of Exchequer Chamber, in which there was great difference of opinion amongst the judges; and in which I venture to think that, after all, an erroneous decision was come to. And I refer you to the case, rather, if I may say so, to warn you against it, than for the sake of any benefit which you may derive from its perusal. The case to which I refer is that of *Muggleton* v. *Barnett* (r). You will find in Appendix A. to my "Principles of the Law of Real Property" (s) an argument, which I do not intend now to repeat, showing the reasons which led me to think that the decision was erroneous in this respect, that the case was decided as if the act to amend the law of inheritance did not affect the question. I had the satisfaction afterwards of finding that my doubts as to the case were shared by so great an authority as Lord St. Leonards,

Muggleton v. *Barnett*.

(r) 1 Hurls. & Norm. 282; and on appeal 2 Hurls. & Norm. 653.

(s) Page 469, 12th ed.

who, in his second edition of his work on the Real Property Statutes (*t*), thus writes, "In the result the Exchequer and Exchequer Chamber, with much diversity of opinion as to the extent of the custom, decided the case against the claimant, who claimed as heir by the custom to the last purchaser, which he was; because he was not heir by the custom to the person last seised. And yet the act extends to all customary tenures, and alters the descent in all such cases, as well as in descents by the common law, by substituting the last purchaser as the stock from whom the descent is to be traced for the person last seised. The court perhaps hardly explained the grounds upon which they held the statute not to apply to this case."

Descent to married woman.

The Married Women's Property Act, stat. 33 & 34 Victoria, c. 93, provides (*u*) that where any freehold, copyhold or customaryhold property shall descend upon any woman, married after the passing of that act, as heiress or co-heiress of an intestate, the rents and profits of such property shall, subject and without prejudice to the trusts of any settlement affecting the same, belong to such woman *for her separate use*, and her receipts alone shall be a good discharge for the same.

Bare trustee.

It is provided by the Land Transfer Act, 1875 (*x*), that, upon the death of a bare trustee intestate as to any corporeal or incorporeal hereditament, of which such trustee was seised in fee simple, such hereditament shall vest, like a chattel real, in the legal personal representative from time to time of such trustee, that is, in his executors or administrators. But the enactment is not to apply to any lands registered under that act. This attempted amendment appears to me to be too partial and uncertain to be of any benefit.

(*t*) Page 271.

(*u*) Sect. 8.

(*x*) Stat. 38 & 39 Vict. c. 87, s. 48.

Proposed abolition of inheritance.

I confess that, saving estates tail, the descent of which should, I think, be permitted to remain, I should be glad to see the whole law of inheritance swept away. The time has gone by when the eldest son was rightly selected, because he was probably stronger and more fit to bear arms than any of his younger brothers. The same principle of military service, which excluded the younger brothers, seems also to have led to the preference of males to females throughout the whole course of the law of descent. It seems to me that, when a man has the misfortune to die intestate, the law should, as far as it can, do for him what it may be supposed he would himself have done, had he made a will. This of course can only be done approximately; but it seems to me that the best approximation would be, to vest his landed property in a real representative, in trust to sell it, and to distribute the proceeds of the same amongst his next of kin, in the same manner as, with regard to personal estate, the executor or administrator of the effects of the deceased sells the same, and distributes the proceeds according to the statute of distribution. I do not think that this would be so violent a change as might at first sight be supposed. Intestacy does not often happen; though, when it does happen, it sometimes occasions great hardship. Settlements and entails would still go on; and, in default of any disposition by the deceased, the law would at any rate attempt to make a beneficial disposition of his property amongst his wife and children or his next of kin, instead of regulating its devolution according to ancient maxims, which have long ceased to be founded on practical reason or justice.

If, however, this change should be thought too violent, it seems to me that, at any rate, it would be most desirable that a real representative should be

Real representative desirable.

appointed for the purpose of paying debts and other charges on the inheritance, subject to which, in so many cases, the lands of an intestate descend to his heir-at-law.

The subject of our next Lecture will be the seisin of the freehold as it affects conveyance.

LECTURE VII.

We now come to the consideration of seisin of the freehold as it affects CONVEYANCE.

The ancient method of conveyance was the simplest possible—a man who was in possession of land might transfer that possession to another person, to hold to him, his heirs and assigns, by what is called a *Feoffment with livery of seisin.* Livery of seisin simply means the delivery of the feudal possession; and this was done by the actual delivery of some symbol, such as a piece of turf, or the branch of a tree, or the key of a door. It was not, however, necessary that the article delivered should be anything concerning the land; for it was resolved in one case (*a*) that the delivery of a parchment deed or of a gold ring in the name of seisin, was quite sufficient for the purpose. You will remember that in a former Lecture I endeavoured to point out the difference between *seisin in deed* and *seisin in law.* As there might have been a *seisin in law* or a *seisin in deed*, so there might have been *livery in law* or a *livery in deed.* Livery in deed was actual delivery by a symbol as above-mentioned. Livery in law was performed by the feoffor when not actually on the land or in the house, but being within sight of it, saying to the feoffee "I give you yonder house or land. Go and enter into the same, and take possession of it accordingly." This livery did not transfer the freehold until an actual entry was made into the land or house by the feoffee, because the possession was not delivered to him, but

Feoffment.

Livery in law.

(*a*) *Thoroughgood's case*, 9 Rep. 136 b, 137 b.

only a licence or power was given him by the feoffor to take possession. Therefore if either the feoffor or feoffee died before entry was made, under livery thus given, the livery became void. And in case the feoffee dare not enter upon the land without endangering his life, he was bound to claim the land by going as near to it as he might safely venture; and this was sufficient to vest the possession in him, and to render the livery in law complete, so as to put him in contemplation of law in actual possession of the premises. Where the lands comprised in a feoffment were all in the same county, though in different vills, livery of seisin within one vill in the name of the whole was sufficient; but where the lands lay in different counties, there must have been a livery in each county. Livery in deed might have been given or received by attorney; but the authority to give or receive seisin was required to be by deed; and the livery must have been made during the lifetime of the feoffor, and also during the lifetime of the feoffee, for in each case the power of attorney ceased by the death of his principal. But the attorney was not bound to deliver seisin on the day of the date of the deed; it was sufficient if he delivered it afterwards (*b*).

Claim in lieu of entry.

Livery by attorney.

No other persons must be in possession.

In order to the validity of a feoffment with livery of seisin, it was absolutely necessary that no other than the feoffor should be in the possession of the land. If there were on the land a mere tenant from year to year, the feoffment was void unless he left the premises; but it seems afterwards to have been thought sufficient if, instead of leaving the premises, he assented to the livery. It was held, that if a tenant for years went away and left his goods upon the premises, still the possession was vacant; but if he left a child there the

(*b*) *Freeman* v. *West*, 2 Wils. 167; *Doe* d. *Heale* v. *Rashleigh*, 3 Barn. & Ald. 156.

possession was then held not to be vacant, and so the livery was void. But it was afterwards decided that the fact of a child remaining on the premises did not make the livery void, provided he was not placed there for the purpose of representing some person claiming title to the premises (*c*). **Child left.**

Livery of seisin was generally accompanied by a deed; and when this was the case, and the livery was made by attorney, as it frequently was, it was usual to endorse upon the deed a memorandum that livery of seisin had been given. In the absence, however, of any such indorsement the courts would, in favour of possession, presume, after twenty years, that livery of seisin must have accompanied the deed of feoffment (*d*). It was not, however, absolutely necessary that any deed, nor even any writing, should be executed. A verbal gift was sufficient, if accompanied with livery of seisin (*e*); and a verbal gift to the feoffee, his heirs and assigns, gave him an estate in fee simple. **Deed of feoffment.** **Memorandum of livery of seisin.**

The proper and technical term to be used in a feoffment was the word *give*. When a tenure was created between the feoffor and the feoffee, as it usually was before the passing of the statute of *Quia emptores* (*f*), the acceptance by the feoffor of *homage* from the feoffee was considered as of itself a warranty of the title to the lands in respect of which the homage was done, so long as the tenancy continued by descent in the blood of the first purchaser (*g*). There was frequently, however, an express warranty. And if homage were not taken, **Word *give*.** **Warranty by acceptance of homage.**

(*c*) *Doe* d. *Reed* v. *Taylor*, 5 Barn. & Adol. 575.

(*d*) See *Doe* d. *Wilkins* v. *Marquis of Cleveland*, 9 Barn. & Cres. 864; *Doe* d. *Rowlandson* v. *Wainwright*, 5 Ad. & Ell. 520; *Doe* d. *Lewis* v. *Davies*, 2 Mee. & Wels. 503, 516.

(*e*) *Sharp's case*, 6 Rep. 26a.

(*f*) Statute 18 Edw. 1, c. 1, ante, p. 21.

(*g*) Litt. ss. 143—147.

and the feoffment contained no clause of warranty, still the word *give* in a feoffment of lands to be holden of the feoffor and his heirs, created a warranty which was binding on himself and his heirs. But in a feoffment to hold of the chief lord of the fee, the warranty implied by the word *give* was binding on the feoffor only during his life. This was provided by a statute of the reign of Edward I. (*h*). The warranty during the life of the feoffor, implied by the word *give*, was abolished by the Act to amend the Law of Real Property (*i*).

Warranty by word *give*.

So great stress did the law lay upon the delivery of feudal seisin, that any person, who was in actual possession of land, whether as tenant for years or for life or in tail or otherwise, might, by delivering seisin to a man and his heirs, thereby create an estate in fee simple. This estate, of course, so far as it exceeded the estate of the donor, was an estate by wrong (*j*). The feoffment was therefore said to have a tortious operation. It gave to the feoffee more than the feoffor ought to have given. This did not give the feoffee a good title; for such a feoffment was a cause of forfeiture to the person next in remainder, after the determination of the estate of the feoffor; and he might enter, either at once, or, if he pleased, not till after the determination of the feoffor's estate. Still, until he did enter, the feoffee had an estate by wrong, according to the terms of the feoffment, whether these terms were put into writing or not.

Feoffment by wrong.

If the feoffee should have died whilst in possession, the lands would have descended to his heir; and this descent cast, in legal language *tolled*, or took away the right of entry of the real owner. The heir being in by descent from his ancestor had, even before his entry, a

Descent tolled entry.

(*h*) Stat. 4 Edw. 1, st. 3, c. 6.

(*i*) Stat. 8 & 9 Vict. c. 106, s. 3.

(*j*) Ante, p. 7.

seisin in law, and he could only be ousted by what was called a real action. But the Act for the Limitation of Actions and Suits (*k*) abolished all real actions except ejectment, and provided (*l*) that no descent cast, discontinuance or warranty, which might happen or be made after the 31st of December, 1833, should *toll* or defeat any right of entry or action for the recovery of land. The term *discontinuance* was applied to a feoffment in fee made by a tenant in tail in possession, which was said to discontinue the estate tail, and deprived the issue in tail of their right of entry on their ancestor's decease.

Discontinuance.

The conveyance of a whole manor might have been made by feoffment. A manor, you will remember, consists of demesnes and services:—Of demesnes, or the land left in the possession of the lord; of services, or the services reserved by the lord, when he granted out portions of his lands to freehold tenants and their heirs, to hold of him and his heirs. If the lord of a manor made a feoffment of his demesne lands, by delivering anything whatever to the feoffee, in the name of seisin of the whole manor, the manor, consisting both of the demesnes and of the services, passed to the feoffee (*m*), subject only to this,—that, with respect to the services, they did not pass to the grantee until the tenants of the manor had attorned tenants to him (*n*). But, by the feoffment and attornment of the tenants, the whole manor effectually passed. Not only did the services of the freehold tenants pass by a feoffment of the manor and the attornment of the tenants, but all rights of an incorporeal nature which were appendant or appurtenant thereto passed also, such as an advowson, or the perpetual right of presentation to an ecclesiastical benefice, and rights of common and way over other people's land.

Conveyance of manor.

Attornment of tenants.

(*k*) Stat. 3 & 4 Will. 4, c. 27.
(*l*) Sect. 39.
(*m*) Co. Litt. 121 b.
(*n*) Litt. s. 553.

It seems singular that the lord of a manor should not have been able to convey his seignory, without the attornment of his tenants, and yet that the tenant, without the consent of his lord, should have been able to alienate his lands. You may remember that, in ancient times, the usual method of alienation was by subinfeudation, or the grant of the lands by the tenant to a sub-tenant and his heirs, to be holden of himself and his heirs. But it seems to have been the case, at any rate in the time of Henry III., that, if a tenant chose to transfer the whole of his lands to another, to be holden of the same chief lord as he held himself, he was able to do so without his lord's permission. Although this position has been disputed with much learning (*o*), it seems the better opinion that such was in fact the case (*p*); and that the statute of *Quia emptores* (*q*), which enabled the grant of lands to be held of the same chief lord, was mainly intended to authorize the grant of *part* of the lands to be holden of the chief lord, which grant certainly could not have been made, without the lord's consent, before that statute.

Statute of Frauds.

Writing required.

I have said that no writing was necessary to a feoffment; and this continued to be the law of England down to the passing of the Statute of Frauds (*r*). By this act it was provided, "that all estates in messuages, manors, lands, tenements and hereditaments, made and created by livery and seisin only, or by parol, and not put in writing, and signed by the parties so making and creating the same, or their agents thereunto lawfully authorized by writing, should have the force and effect of leases or estates at will only, and should not, either in law or equity, be deemed or taken to have any other or greater force or effect, any consideration for making

(*o*) Wright's Tenures, 154, 155.

(*p*) Bracton, lib. 2, c. 19; Co. Litt. 43 a.

(*q*) Stat. 18 Edw. 1, c. 1.

(*r*) Stat. 29 Car. 2, c. 3.

such parol leases or estates, or any former law or usage to the contrary notwithstanding."

Still, a deed was unnecessary until an act of the present reign. The Act to amend the Law of Real Property (*s*) now provides (*t*), "that, after the 1st October, 1845, all corporeal tenements and hereditaments shall, as regards the conveyance of the immediate freehold thereof, be deemed to lie in grant as well as in livery;" that is to say, it enables now the owner of a freehold estate to grant that estate by deed, without any livery of seisin; or, if he pleases, he may still make a feoffment with livery of seisin. But the 3rd section goes on to provide, "that a feoffment made after the 1st day of October, 1845, other than a feoffment made under a custom by an infant, shall be void at law, unless evidenced by deed." The exception of a feoffment made under a custom by an infant appears to be pointed to the custom of gavelkind, under which, you will remember, the lands descend to all the sons or all the brothers in equal shares. And it is a part of that custom, that any infant under the age of twenty-one years, may, after he has attained the age of fifteen years, convey his share of the premises by feoffment. If, therefore, the lands be of gavelkind tenure, an infant may now, by virtue of the custom, if he be of the age of fifteen years, make a valid conveyance of his share in the land, by feoffment without a deed.

A deed now required.

The Act to amend the Law of Real Property further provides (*u*), that a feoffment made after the 1st day of October, 1845, shall not have any tortious operation. Any person, therefore, may still make a feoffment, with livery of seisin, if he pleases; but the feoffment must

(*s*) Stat. 8 & 9 Vict. c. 106. (*t*) Sect. 2. (*u*) Sect. 4.

now be evidenced by deed, and it will not have any tortious operation; that is, its effect will be limited to simply conveying to the feoffee such an estate in the land as the feoffor has and may lawfully convey, and nothing further.

A fine.

There is another mode of conveyance not unfrequently used in ancient times, of which some explanation should be given; and that is, *a fine*. A conveyance of land by fine was called levying a fine. It was called a fine from the words with which the record of the fine began; namely, these—"*Hæc est finalis concordia inter, &c.*," This is the final concord between, &c. A fine was in effect a compromise of a suit commenced concerning the lands intended to be conveyed. A writ was sued out, and the parties appeared in court; and a composition of the suit was then entered into, with the consent of the judges, whereby the lands in question were declared to be the right of one of the parties, either with or without the suggestion of a former gift or by a present grant. This agreement was reduced into writing, and was enrolled amongst the records of the court, where it was preserved by the proper officer, and so was not liable to be lost or defaced. And in fact it had the effect of a judgment of the court. On the completion of the fine, a writ was issued to the sheriff of the county in which the land lay, in the same form as if a judgment had been obtained in a hostile suit, directing the sheriff to deliver seisin and possession to the person who acquired the lands. But if he was already in possession this writ was dispensed with (*x*).

Parts of a fine.

A fine consisted of five parts,—namely, the original writ; the licence to agree, or *licencia concordandi*, which was given by the leave of the court, on payment of a fine to the king, called the king's silver. The third part was the concord or agreement, by which it was agreed

(*x*) Cruise on Fines, 63, 64.

that the lands were the right of the person in whose favour the fine was levied. The fourth part was a note of the proceedings, drawn up by an officer, called the chirographer; and the fifth part was the *chirograph* of the fine, which included the whole matter. This chirograph was delivered to the parties, and was legal evidence of the fine, and was retained by the purchaser as one of his title deeds. Chirograph.

One advantage of a fine was this. If a man made a feoffment of his manor (*y*), we have seen that the services of his freehold tenants did not pass to the feoffee, unless they chose to attorn to him; but if he conveyed his manor by fine, the services of the tenants passed to the person whom the fine declared to be entitled to the lands; for the fine was a judicial proceeding and conveyed a seisin in law prior to attornment, though before attornment the purchaser could not distrain for the services due (*z*).

Services of tenants passed by fine.

However, a statute of the reign of Queen Anne (*a*), has now rendered all attornments unnecessary. The act provides (*b*) that after the first day of Trinity Term, 1706, all grants and conveyances, by fine or otherwise, of any manors or rents, or of the reversion or remainder of any messuages or lands, shall be good and effectual to all intents and purposes, without any attornment of the tenants of any such manors, or of the land out of which such rent shall be issuing, or of the particular tenants upon whose particular estates any such reversions or remainders shall and may be expectant or depending, as if their attornment had been had and made. Provided nevertheless (*c*) that no such tenant shall be prejudiced or damaged by payment of any rent

Attornment abolished.

(*y*) Ante, p. 103.
(*z*) Litt. s. 579.
(*a*) Stat. 4 & 5 Anne, c. 16.
(*b*) Sect. 9.
(*c*) Sect. 10.

to any such grantor or conusor, or by breach of any condition for non-payment of rent before notice shall be given to him of such grant by the conusee or grantee.

Fine by married woman.

Another advantage of a fine was this, that it enabled a married woman to join with her husband in making a conveyance of her lands, which she could not otherwise do. For, by the common law, she was unable, by any means, to deprive herself of her own inheritance. But as a fine was a judicial procedure, and had the effect of a judgment, a married woman was as effectually barred by a fine, as by a judgment in an adverse suit. The wife, moreover, whenever a fine was levied, was examined separately from her husband, in order to ascertain whether she consented of her own free will to the conveyance intended to be made.

Wife was separately examined.

Fine sur conusance de droit come ceo, &c.

There were four sorts of fines. The first and most usual was a fine *sur conusance* (or *cognizance*) *de droit come ceo qu'il ad de son done*, that is, a fine on acknowledgment of right, as that which he has of his gift. I should mention that the person who levied the fine was called the cognisor or conusor, and the person to whom the fine was levied was called the cognisee or conusee; and a fine of this nature was an acknowledgment of the right of the cognisee to the premises in question, as that which the cognisee had of the gift or feoffment of the cognisor, and it was used for the conveyance of an estate in fee simple, and nothing but an absolute freehold could pass by it. The next kind of fine was a fine *sur cognizance de droit tantum*. This was upon an acknowledgment of right only; and this kind of fine was used for passing a reversionary interest, such as a reversion or remainder expectant upon an estate of freehold; for, as we have seen, there could be no feoffment with livery of seisin of any such reversion or remainder, so long as the estate of the tenant for life

Fine sur conusance de droit tantum.

endured. The third kind of fine was called a fine *sur concessit*, by which the cognisor, in order to make an end to all disputes, granted to the cognisee a new estate by way of supposed composition, which estate might be either in fee, in tail, for life, or for years. But it was generally used, when it was used, which was not very often, for granting an estate for years only. The fourth kind of fine was a double fine, and had the effect of the fine *sur cognizance de droit come ceo, &c.*, and the fine *sur concessit*. It was called a fine *sur done grant et render*. It had, in fact, the effect of a feoffment and reinfeoffment, and gave a new estate.

Fine sur concessit.

Fine sur done, grant et render.

Fines had also another use. They put an end to all adverse claims to the land after a certain period. The statute of 18 Edward I. statute 4, called the statute *Modus levandi fines*, not only provided for the examination of a married woman before four justices, and that if she did not assent to the fine it should not be levied; but it also declared that a fine was of so great force, and of so strong nature, that it concluded not only such as were parties and privies to the fine, and their heirs, but all other people in the world, being of full age, out of prison, of whole memory, and within the four seas the day of the fine levied, if they made not their claim of their action within a year and a day. This was found to be too short a period of limitation, and it was repealed by a statute of Edward III. (*d*). But subsequent statutes of the time of Richard III. and Henry VII. revived the power of a fine to bar adverse claims. These statutes were the 1 Richard III. c. 7, and 4 & 5 Henry VII. c. 24. By these statutes, however, the time for adverse claim was extended to five years; and it was provided by the last statute, that after the engrossing of every fine to be levied in the King's Court, before the Justices of Common Place,

No claim after fines.

Proclamations.

(*d*) Stat. 34 Edw. 3, c. 16.

of any lands, tenements or other hereditaments, the same fine should be openly and solemnly read and proclaimed in the same court the same term, and in three terms then next following, of four several days in every term; and on the same time that it was so read and proclaimed all pleas were to cease. These proclamations having been found inconveniently numerous, it was provided, by a statute of Elizabeth (*e*), that a fine should be proclaimed only four times, one in the term in which it was engrossed, and once in every of the three terms afterwards. This proclamation so made had the effect of concluding all strangers, as well as those who were party or privy to the fine, unless they pursued their title by way of action or lawful entry within five years; or, if they were under any legal incapacity, then within five years next after the removal of such incapacity. If, as sometimes happened, the fine was not proclaimed, it had no effect in barring adverse claims not made within five years. A statute of the present reign (*f*) provides retrospectively that all fines heretofore levied in the Court of Common Pleas, shall be conclusively deemed to have been levied with proclamations, and shall have the force and effect of fines with proclamations.

Fines had also the effect of barring the heirs of the body of a person to whom an estate tail had been granted. Of this I shall say more when I come to consider the seisin of the freehold as it affects settlements.

Difference between feoffment and fine.

There was this difference between a feoffment and a fine. A feoffment by a tenant at will or a tenant for years to A. and his heirs created a tortious fee-simple in A. by reason of the actual delivery of the seisin. But a fine levied by a tenant at will or a tenant for years

(*e*) Stat. 31 Eliz. c. 2. (*f*) Stat. 11 & 12 Vict. c. 70.

to a conusee who had no estate of freehold in the premises was void as against the owner of the freehold. For a fine implied a previous feoffment; and the law would never imply a wrongful act. If, therefore, a tenant for years wished to acquire the fee-simple, his proper plan was, first, to make a feoffment, and then to levy a fine. By the feoffment a tortious fee was created; and by the fine the owner of the reversion was barred if he did not enter for the forfeiture committed within five years after the fine was levied, or, if he pleased, within five years after the time when the tenant's term of years would regularly have expired.

Acquisition of fee simple by tenant for years.

All fines, however, are now abolished. This was effected by the Act for the Abolition of Fines and Recoveries, and for the substitution of more simple modes of assurance (*g*). We shall speak of recoveries by-and-bye. The act enacts (*h*) that, after the 31st day of December, 1833, no fine shall be levied of lands of any tenure, except where a writ should have been sued out on or before that day. The power which a fine had to convey the estate of a married woman having of course ceased by the abolition of fines, a substitution for this power was provided by the 77th and following sections of that act. By these it is provided that, after the 31st day of December, 1833, it shall be lawful for every married woman, in every case, except that of being a tenant in tail, for which provision had already been made by the act, by deed to dispose of lands of any tenure and money subject to be invested in the purchase of lands, and also to dispose of, release, surrender or extinguish any estate which she alone, or she and her husband in her right, may have in any lands of any tenure, or in any such money as aforesaid, and also to release or extinguish any power which may be vested in or limited or reserved to her in regard to

Fines now abolished.

Power of married woman to dispose of lands.

(*g*) Stat. 3 & 4 Will. 4, c. 74. (*h*) Sect. 2.

any lands of any tenure, or any such money as aforesaid, or in regard to any estate in lands of any tenure, or in any such money as aforesaid, as fully and effectually as she could do if she were a *feme sole;* save and except that no such disposition, release, surrender or extinguishment shall be valid and effectual, unless the husband concur in the deed by which the same shall be effected, nor unless the deed be acknowledged by her as thereinafter directed. The act then provides (*i*) that every deed to be executed by a married woman for any of the purposes of the act (except as to her consent as protector to the disposition of a tenant in tail) shall, upon her executing the same or afterwards, be produced and *acknowledged* by her, as her act and deed, before a judge of one of the superior courts at Westminster, or a master in chancery, or before two of the perpetual commissioners, or two special commissioners to be appointed as thereby provided. And it is enacted (*k*) that such judge, master in chancery, or commissioners as aforesaid, before he or they shall receive the acknowledgment by any married woman of any deed, by which any disposition, release, surrender or extinguishment shall be made by her under that act, shall examine her apart from her husband touching her knowledge of such deed, and shall ascertain whether she freely and voluntarily consents to such deed; and, unless she freely and voluntarily consents to such deed, shall not permit her to acknowledge the same; and, in such case, such deed shall, so far as relates to the execution thereof by such married woman, be void. The act provides (*l*) for the issuing of a commission to take the acknowledgment of a married woman in cases where, by reason of residence beyond seas or ill-health, or any other sufficient cause, she shall be prevented from making the acknowledgment required by the act. The deed, when acknowledged, has

Husband to concur.

Acknowledgment.

Separate examination of married woman.

Commission to take acknowledgment.

(*i*) Sect. 79.

(*k*) Sect. 80.

(*l*) Sect. 83.

an indorsement thereon, which is directed (*m*), to be to the following effect, namely:—"This deed marked (here add some letter or other mark for the purpose of identification) was this day produced before me and acknowledged by (so and so), therein named to be her act and deed; previous to which acknowledgment the said (so and so) was examined by me, separately and apart from her husband, touching her knowledge of the contents of the said deed and her consent thereto, and declared the same to be freely and voluntarily executed by her." This is to be signed by the person taking the acknowledgment. The person taking the acknowledgment is also required to sign a certificate of the taking of such acknowledgment, to be written or engrossed on a separate piece of parchment, which certificate is to be to the effect of a form given in the act. Sect. 85 provides that this certificate, together with an affidavit by some person verifying the same, and the signature thereof by the party by whom the same shall purport to be signed, is to be lodged with the officer of the Court of Common Pleas at Westminster, now represented by the Common Pleas Division of the High Court of Justice; who is to file the same of record. And sect. 86 provides that when the certificate shall be so filed of record, the deed so acknowledged shall, so far as regards the disposition, release, surrender or extinguishment made by any married woman, whose acknowledgment shall be so certified, take effect from the time of its being acknowledged; and the subsequent filing of the certificate is to have relation to such acknowledgment. The certificate is essential, and the memorandum of acknowledgment indorsed on the deed is insufficient without it. This was decided by the Court of Exchequer in the case of *Jolly* v. *Handcock* (*n*). The officer with whom the certificates are lodged is required (*o*)

Indorsement on deed acknowledged.

Certificate of acknowledgment.

Filing of certificate in office of Common Pleas Division.

(*m*) Sect. 84.

(*n*) 7 Exch. 820.

(*o*) Sect. 87.

to make and keep an index of the same, which index shall contain the names of the married women and their husbands, alphabetically arranged, and the dates of such certificates, and of the deeds to which the same shall respectively relate, and such other particulars as shall be found convenient; and every such certificate shall be entered in the index, as soon as may be after such certificate shall have been filed. It is further provided (*p*), that after the filing of any such certificate as aforesaid, the officer, with whom the certificate shall be lodged, shall at any time deliver a copy, signed by him, of any such certificate, to any person applying for such copy; and every such copy shall be received as evidence of the acknowledgment of the deed, to which such certificate shall refer.

Index of acknowledgments.

Office copy of certificate.

The 91st section provides, that if a husband shall, in consequence of being a lunatic, idiot, or of unsound mind, and whether he shall have been found such by inquisition or not, or shall from any other cause be incapable of executing a deed, or of making a surrender of lands held by copy of court roll, or if his residence shall not be known, or he shall be in prison, or shall be living apart from his wife, either by mutual consent or by sentence of divorce, or in consequence of his being transported beyond the seas, or from any other cause whatsoever, it shall be lawful for the Court of Common Pleas at Westminster (now represented by the Common Pleas Division of the High Court), by an order to be made in a summary way upon the application of the wife, and upon such evidence as to the said Court shall seem meet, to dispense with the concurrence of the husband in any case in which his concurrence is required by the act or otherwise; and all acts, deeds or surrenders to be done, executed, or made by the wife,

Husband incapable, absent, &c.

Concurrence dispensed with.

(*p*) Sect. 88.

in pursuance of such order, in regard to lands of any tenure, or in regard to money subject to be invested in the purchase of lands, shall be done, executed, or made by her in the same manner as if she were a *feme sole*, and when done, executed, or made by her shall (but without prejudice to the rights of the husband as then existing independently of the act) be as good and valid as they would have been if the husband had concurred. Where a married woman has obtained an order of this kind, there is no necessity for her to acknowledge the deed as above provided (*q*).

Disclaimer.

The act to which I have before referred for the amendment of the law of real property (*r*) enables a married woman to *disclaim* by deed duly acknowledged with the concurrence of her husband, any estate or interest in any tenements or hereditaments in England of any tenure, which she may not choose to accept. Another statute (*s*) removes doubts which might otherwise arise as to the validity of any deed acknowledged before a judge, master, or commissioner, who may be interested either as a party, or as the solicitor, or clerk to the solicitor, of one of the parties, or otherwise, in the transaction giving occasion for such acknowledgment. The power of taking acknowledgments of married women has, by another statute of the present reign (*t*), been extended to judges of the County Courts.

County court judges.

Questionable benefit of wife's separate acknowledgment.

I think that it may well be doubted whether the elaborate machinery thus provided for the protection of married women is of any practical benefit. Certainly it always appears to be the object of married women and their advisers to escape from the protection which this

(*q*) *Goodchild* v. *Dougal*, M. R., L. R., 3 Ch. Div. 650.

(*r*) Stat. 8 & 9 Vict. c. 106, s. 7; ante, p. 105.

(*s*) Stat. 17 & 18 Vict. c. 75.

(*t*) Stat. 19 & 20 Vict. c. 108, s. 73.

act affords them. Their endeavour is so to settle their lands that they may dispose of them, sometimes with the concurrence of their husbands, sometimes without; but always without the expense and trouble of a separate examination.

The Vendor and Purchaser Act, 1874 (*u*), enacts that where any freehold or copyhold hereditament shall be vested in a married woman as a bare trustee, she may convey or surrender the same as if she were a *feme sole.*

The power which a fine had to quiet a title after five years' non-claim, was taken away when fines were prohibited to be levied; and no substitution for the effect of fines in this respect was enacted by the act by which fines were abolished. This was done of purpose; for it was thought that five years was too short a time of limitation of adverse suits; and, in the same session of parliament, the act was passed which is now in force, "For the limitation of Actions and Suits relating to Real Property and for simplifying the remedies for trying the rights thereto (*x*)." It is not my purpose now to go into all the provisions of this act. Suffice it to say, that the term limited by that act is, generally speaking, twenty years next after the time that possession or receipt once had shall have been discontinued, or within ten years after the cesser of any disability.

Statute of Limitation.

A new statute of limitations has recently been passed (*y*); but this statute does not come into operation until the 1st January, 1879. This act, when it comes into operation, is to alter the period of twenty years to twelve years, and ten years to six years next after the cesser of any disability.

New Statute of Limitations.

(*u*) Stat. 37 & 38 Vict. c. 78, s. 6.

(*x*) Stat. 3 & 4 Will. 4, c. 27.

(*y*) Stat. 37 & 38 Vict. c. 57.

LECTURE VIII.

THERE were certain cases under the ancient law, in which livery of seisin was unnecessary to the passing of an estate of freehold. The first was the case of *coparceners*, who, under the old law, might make partition between themselves, as well by parol or word of mouth, without a deed, as by a deed with livery of seisin. Parceners were said to have a threefold privity; viz. in estate, in person, and in possession, and, by the common law, were always able to make partition between themselves. Coparceners.

Again *joint tenants* might make partition between themselves of the lands of which they were joint tenants, without any feoffment and livery of seisin from one to the other; and in fact in this case livery of seisin was improper. Joint tenants are persons to whom lands are given, to hold to them their heirs and assigns jointly; or there may be joint tenants for life only; but they are said to have a privity in estate and in possession. Where there are two joint tenants, each is said to be seised *per mie et per tout;* so that, each being seised, the proper conveyance from one joint tenant to another is by a deed of release. By such a deed a joint tenant is released of all right of his companion, and holds the land released to himself in severalty. Joint tenants in fact are considered by law as one person for most purposes; and, on the decease of one of them, the whole survives to the survivors or survivor; and, on the decease of the survivor intestate, goes to his heirs, to the exclusion of the heirs of any of the previously deceased joint tenants. Joint tenants.

Tenants in common.

Tenants in common are persons who have distinct and several interests in their undivided shares. They have a privity only in possession, and not in estate; and the consequence is that, if one tenant in common wishes to convey his estate to another tenant in common, he must do it, not by a release, but by a proper conveyance. This proper conveyance, in ancient times, was a feoffment with livery of seisin. The Act to amend the Law of Real Property (*a*), however, now provides (*b*)—that a partition of any tenements or hereditaments made after the 1st October, 1845, shall be void at law unless made by deed. The Statute of Frauds (*c*) had previously provided that all estates of freehold, made or created by parol, and not put in writing, should have no greater effect than leases or estates at will only.

Partition now void unless made by deed.

Another exception to the rule, which required livery of seisin to pass an estate of freehold, anciently occurred in the case of an *exchange* of lands between one person and another. Littleton says (*d*), "And in some cases a man shall have by the grant of another a fee simple, fee tail, or freehold without livery of seisin. As, if there be two men, and each of them is seised of one quantity of land in one county, and the one granteth his land to the other in exchange for the land the other hath; and in like manner the other granteth his land to the first grantor, in exchange for the land which the first grantor hath; in this case each may enter into the other's land, so put in exchange, without any livery of seisin; and such exchange, made by parol, of tenements in the same county without writing is good enough." But if the lands were within divers counties, then a deed indented made between them was required. If, however, both parties to the exchange died before the entry of either of them into the lands given to him in

Exchange.

(*a*) Stat. 8 & 9 Vict. c. 106.
(*b*) Sect. 3.
(*c*) 29 Car. 2, c. 3; ante, p. 104.
(*d*) Sect. 62.

exchange, then the exchange became void. But if one entered, and the other afterwards died before having entered into his portion, his heir had a right to enter in the place of his ancestor.

Every partition and exchange formerly implied a warranty by the party who gave up, in the one case a share of the lands, and in the other lands in exchange, of the title to that which he gave up. It was a condition of every warranty that in case the person to whom the warranty was made were evicted, he should receive lands of equal value from the warrantor. But the Act to amend the Law of Real Property (*e*) now provides(*f*), that an exchange or a partition of any tenements or hereditaments, made by deed executed after the 1st day of October, 1845, shall not imply any condition in law. It also provides (*g*) that an exchange, as well as a partition, of any tenements or hereditaments, not being copyhold, shall be void at law unless made by deed.

Implied warranty on partition or exchange.

Another exception to the rule requiring livery of seisin occurred in cases where a release might be made by deed. Thus, one coparcener (*h*) could convey to another either by feoffment with livery of seisin or by deed of release; joint tenants, as we have seen (*i*), could only convey to one another by deed of release. So the owner of the fee simple may convey his estate, and with it the seisin of the freehold, to his tenant at will, or to his tenant for years, if in possession, by a deed of release. This deed of release is said to operate in this case by way of enlargement of the tenant's estate; and it requires words of limitation, that is, words marking out the increased estate which the tenant is to have by virtue of the release whether in tail, or in fee simple.

Release.

Release by way of enlargement.

(*e*) Stat. 8 & 9 Vict. c. 106.
(*f*) Sect. 4.
(*g*) Sect. 3.
(*h*) Ante, p. 117.
(*i*) Ante, p. 117.

A release to a tenant who has not entered into the lands is void. The release can only be to a person in possession of the lands; but to such person the conveyance of the lands themselves may be made by a release, which, as I have said, passes the seisin of the freehold, and operates by way of enlargement of his estate. This kind of release by way of enlargement was, until lands were rendered grantable by deed, constantly employed in conveyancing, as we shall hereafter see. The law on this subject is thus laid down by Littleton (*k*): "Also, if a man letteth to another his land for term of years, if the lessor release to the lessee all his right, &c., before that the lessee had entered into the same land by force of the same lease, such release is void; for that the lessee had not possession in the land at the time of the release made, but only a right to have the same land by force of the lease. But if the lessee enter into the land, and hath possession of it by force of the said lease, then such release made to him by the feoffor, or by his heir, is sufficient to him, by reason of the privity which, by force of the lease, is between them."

Release by way of extinguishment.

Again there may be a release by way of extinguishment; such as a release of rents or services due from the releasee to the releasor. Thus the lord of a manor may release his seignory to any of his freehold tenants; and such a release will operate as an extinguishment of the seignory; so that the tenant will then hold of the next lord paramount. So a right of entry into lands of which another man is seised may be extinguished by a deed of release. The law of release by deed is the same now as it anciently was.

Right of entry.

Confirmation.

There might also have been, and there may be still, a *confirmation* of a voidable estate by a deed executed by the person in whose favour the estate is voidable.

(*k*) Sect. 459.

Again, if there be a tenant for life in possession of land, he may give up his estate and interest in the land, and with it the seisin of the freehold, to the person next in remainder or reversion. This giving up is called a *surrender* of his estate. Anciently such a surrender might have been made by mere parol or word of mouth. Coke says (*l*), that the reason why an estate for life in lands might be surrendered without deed, and without livery of seisin, was, because it is but the yielding or a restoring of the estate again to him in the immediate reversion or remainder, which is always favoured at law. The Statute of Frauds (*m*), however, as we have seen (*n*), required all conveyances of every sort to be put into writing. And the Act to amend the Law of Real Property (*o*) now provides (*p*), that a surrender in writing of an interest in any tenements or hereditaments, not being a copyhold interest, and not being an interest which might by law have been created without writing, made after the 1st day of October, 1845, shall be void at law unless made by deed. A tenant for years may surrender his estate for years to the next immediate remainderman or reversioner in the same manner as a tenant for life.

Surrender by tenant for life.

Surrender by tenant for years.

Another exception to the rule requiring livery of seisin occurred in the case of a *grant*. Everything of which it was impossible to make livery of seisin, but which the law permitted to be aliened, was required to be conveyed by deed of grant. It was said that corporeal hereditaments lay in livery, and incorporeal hereditaments lay in grant. Therefore the owner of a reversion or remainder of lands, the possession or seisin of which belonged to the particular tenant, or owner of the first estate, was enabled to convey his reversion or remainder

Grant.

(*l*) Co. Litt. 338 a.
(*m*) Stat. 29 Car. 2, c. 3.
(*n*) Ante, p. 104.
(*o*) Stat. 8 & 9 Vict. c. 106.
(*p*) Sect. 3.

by a deed of grant. So a lord of a manor might convey any seignory, with its incidental rent, without his demesnes, by a deed of grant. But, in each of these cases, the attornment of the tenant in possession was required to be made prior to the abolition of attornment by the statute of Anne (q), to which I referred in my last Lecture (r). In like manner anything appendant or appurtenant to land, such as an advowson belonging to a manor, might be severed from the manor by a deed of grant; and in that case it became an incorporeal hereditament *in gross*, as it was called, that is, separate and distinct from the manor, and alienable by a deed of grant. So there might be a right of common in gross: that is, not exercised in respect of any particular lands; and such a right could only be aliened by a deed of grant. So a right of sporting is an incorporeal hereditament, and can only be conveyed by deed of grant (s).

Attornment.

Severance of appendants or appurtenances.

Advowson in gross.

Common in gross.

Right of sporting.

There were some rights which, under the ancient law, were not alienable in any manner, except so far as this, that, in some cases, they might be simply extinguished and put an end to. One of these rights was a right of entry into lands, which right might have been released to the person seised of the freehold, or in possession as tenant for years (t), but could not have been transferred to another person. This was found very inconvenient in the cases of leases to tenants reserving to the landlord a right of re-entry in case of non-payment of rent, or non-observance or non-performance of the covenants contained in the lease. A remedy was accordingly provided by a statute of the reign of King Henry VIII. (u). This statute recites that before that time divers, as well

Inalienable rights.

Right of entry.

Conditions of re-entry in leases.

Stat. 32 Hen. VIII. c. 34.

(q) Stat. 4 & 5 Anne, c. 16, s. 9.

(r) Ante, p. 107.

(s) See *Bird* v. *Higginson*, 6 Ad. & Ell. 824; *Thomas* v. *Fredricks*, 10 Q. B. 775.

(t) Ante, p. 120.

(u) Stat. 32 Hen. 8, c. 34.

temporal as ecclesiastical and religious persons, had made sundry leases, demises and grants to divers other persons of sundry manors, &c., and other hereditaments for term of life or lives or for term of years, by writing under their seal or seals, containing certain conditions, covenants and agreements to be performed, as well on the part and behalf of the said lessees and grantees, their executors and assigns, as on the behalf of the said lessors and grantors, their heirs and successors; and forasmuch as by the common law of this realm, no stranger to any covenant, action or condition, shall take any advantage or benefit of the same by any means or ways in the law, but only such as be parties or privies thereunto, by reason whereof grantees of reversions were excluded to have any entry or action against the lessees for breach of any condition, covenant, or agreement comprised in the indentures of their leases. And it enacts that all persons and bodies politic, their heirs, successors and assigns, who had any gift or grant from the Crown, by letters patent, of lands which belonged to the suppressed monasteries, or which by any other means came to the king's hands, as also all other persons, being grantees or assignees to or by the king, or to or by any other person or persons than the king, and the heirs, executors, successors and assigns of every of them, should and might have and enjoy like advantages against the lessees, their executors, administrators and assigns, by entry for non-payment of the rent, or for doing of waste, or other forfeiture, and also should and might have and enjoy all and every such like and the same advantages, benefits and remedies, by action only, for not performing of their conditions, covenants or agreements contained and expressed in the indentures of their said leases, demises or grants, against all and every the said lessees and former grantees, their executors, administrators and assigns, as the said lessors or grantors themselves or their heirs or successors ought, should or might have had and enjoyed at any time or times.

Object of this statute.

The main object of this enactment was to enable persons, to whom the Crown had made grants of the lands of monasteries which had then been dissolved, to enforce against their tenants the covenants and conditions contained in their leases; but you will observe that it extends to all other persons, and it is by virtue of this act that, if a person leases his land by deed with a condition of re-entry on non-payment of rent or non-performance of covenants, and then sells it subject to his tenant's interest, the purchaser may now, in case of default in payment of rent or performance of covenants, enforce against the tenant the condition of re-entry contained in his lease. But the act does not extend to any breach of the conditions made before the grant of the reversion to the grantee. The act applies only to leases by deed (*v*).

Right of entry, &c. anciently inalienable.

A right of entry, not expectant upon the determination of a lease, still remained inalienable. In like manner a contingent interest in land, or what is called an executory interest, that is, an interest to arise at a future time or on a given event, and the possibility of having lands at some future time, in consequence of a gift, for instance, to a class of persons to be ascertained at a future time of which probably the owner of the possibility might be one, could not anciently have been aliened by deed; although it might have been extinguished by release to the owner of the freehold, or by a fine levied by the owner of any such contingent or future interest or possibility; and in some cases these rights might have been bound in equity by a contract respecting them.

(*v*) *Standen* v. *Christmas*, 10 Q. B. 135.

Contingent interests, possibilities, rights of entry, &c., now alienable.

But the Act to amend the Law of Real Property (*x*) has now enacted (*y*) that, after the 1st day of October, 1845, a contingent, an executory and a future interest, and a possibility coupled with an interest, in any tenements or hereditaments of any tenure, whether the object of the gift, or limitation of such interest or possibility, be or be not ascertained, also a right of entry, whether immediate or future, and whether vested or contingent, into or upon any tenements or hereditaments in England of any tenure, may be disposed of by deed; and that every such disposition by a married woman shall be conformable to the provisions, relative to dispositions by married women, of the Act for the Abolition of Fines and Recoveries and for the Substitution of more simple Modes of Assurance (*z*), or in Ireland of the Act for the Abolition of Fines and Recoveries and for the Substitution of more simple Modes of Assurance in Ireland (*a*).

Exception.

This act has been held by the Court of Exchequer not to apply to a right of entry under a condition in a lease, *broken before the alienation* of the reversion, but only to an original right, where there has been a disseisin, or where the party has a right to recover lands, and his right of entry and nothing but that remains (*b*). It seems, therefore, that the assignee of the reversion expectant on the determination of a lease, though he may take advantage of breaches of condition in the lease which may occur in his own time, cannot have assigned to him any right to enter in respect of breaches which occurred previously to the assignment of the reversion to him. And so it has been held by the Court of Queen's Bench (*c*).

(*x*) Stat. 8 & 9 Vict. c. 106.

(*y*) Sect. 6.

(*z*) Stat. 3 & 4 Will. 4, c. 74; ante, pp. 111—114.

(*a*) Stat. 4 & 5 Will. 4, c. 92.

(*b*) *Hunt* v. *Bishop*, 8 Ex. 675, 680; affirmed on appeal, *Hunt* v. *Remnant*, 9 Ex. 635.

(*c*) *Crane* v. *Batten*, 22 Law Times, 220.

For many years feoffments, fines, and deeds of release, confirmation, surrender or grant, with occasionally common recoveries, of which we shall speak hereafter, comprised the whole of the machinery for the conveyance of land; but in the reign of King Henry VIII. a famous statute was passed, called the Statute of Uses (*d*), which effected a complete revolution in the whole system of conveyancing. I think it will be more convenient if I postpone the consideration of conveyance by virtue of that statute to my next Lecture, and proceed now to consider the alienation of copyhold lands.

Statute of Uses.

Copyholder.

A copyholder, as you will remember, is in law only a tenant at will: he has not the feudal seisin or possession. The feudal seisin is, by virtue of the possession of the copyholder, vested in the lord of the manor (*e*); but, by custom, the copyholder may have a *quasi seisin* or possession of the lands he holds, analogous to the seisin which a freehold tenant has of the lands held by him. Copyholds, as I said in a former Lecture (*f*), pass by surrender and admittance. A copyhold tenant, who wishes to alienate his lands, surrenders them, generally by means of delivering a rod, to the lord or his steward, to the use of the person in whose favour he wishes the conveyance to be made; and this person is then admitted tenant to the lord pursuant to the surrender. After he has been admitted, but not before, he is said to be *seised* (though this only a *quasi seisin*) of his copyhold tenements. Before admission he has nothing but a right to be admitted, and no quasi seisin at all. After admission he is seised at the will of the lord, according to the custom of the manor, of the lands to which he has been admitted, for such an estate as has

Surrender and admittance.

(*d*) Stat. 27 Hen. 8, c. 10.
(*e*) Ante, p. 35.
(*f*) Ante, p. 47.

been limited or marked out by the surrender, in pursuance of which the admission has been made. If the tenant of a copyhold tenement, holden for a customary estate in fee simple, should die intestate leaving a customary heir, his heir, on entry, will have a *quasi seisin* before his admission. But the lord may require him to take admission, as on every admission the lord is usually entitled to a fine.

In analogy, however, to the law of freeholds, which permitted a person, who had merely a right of entry or other right to land of which another was seised, to release his right by deed to that other person, the law allows a person who has a right to copyholds, to which another person has been admitted, to release that right to him by a deed of release, similar to a deed of release of a right in freehold lands. It was at one time questioned whether such a release by deed of copyholds was valid; on this ground, that as copyholds passed by surrender and admission, the title to them appears on the court rolls of the manor; whereas, a deed of this kind, not being a transaction entered on the court rolls, would be in fact a title-deed of copyholds not appearing of record on the rolls. It was, however, decided in *Kitė and Queinton's case* (*g*), that such a right in copyholds might lawfully be released by deed to the copyhold tenant.

Release of right by deed.

When a married woman was entitled to copyhold lands, she was enabled, by the ordinary law of copyholds, to surrender the same, with the concurrence of her husband, she being separately examined by the steward of the manor touching her knowledge of the contents of the surrender and her free consent thereto. The Act for the Abolition of Fines and Recoveries, and for the Substitution of more simple Modes of Assur-

Copyholds of married woman.

(*g*) 4 Co. Rep. 25 a.

ance (*h*) accordingly provides (*i*), that that act shall not extend to lands held by copy of court roll of or to which a married woman, or she and her husband in her right, may be seised or entitled for an estate at law, in any case in which any of the objects to be effected by that clause could, before the passing of the act, have been effected by her, in concurrence with her husband, by surrender into the hands of the lord of the manor of which the lands may be parcel.

Trust of copyholds for married woman.

This provision, you will see, extends only to lands of which a married woman, and her husband in her right, may be seised or entitled for an estate at law. Copyholds may be held in trust for a married woman and her customary heirs. In this case there was some doubt, before the act, how an alienation of her equitable interest in these copyholds could be made by her. The 77th section of the act (*j*), however, now extends to lands of any tenure, including of course copyholds, with the single exception of an estate at law, of which a married woman may be seised. So, that, under that section, she and her husband may dispose of her equitable estate in copyholds by deed executed by her with her husband's concurrence, and acknowledged by her under the provision of that act. Or, if she pleases, she may convey her estate by surrender and admittance, in the same manner as if her estate were an estate at law and not in equity. For the 90th section of the act provides that in every case in which a husband and wife shall, either in or out of court, surrender into the hands of the lord of a manor, any lands held by copy of court roll parcel of the manor, and in which she alone, or she and her husband in her right, may have an *equitable estate*, the wife shall, upon such surrender being made, be separately examined by the person taking the surrender,

(*h*) Stat. 3 & 4 Will. 4, c. 74.
(*i*) Sect. 77.
(*j*) Ante, p. 111.

in the same manner as she would have been, if the estate to which she alone, or she and her husband in her right, may be entitled in such lands, were an estate at law, instead of a mere estate in equity. And every such surrender, when such examination shall be taken, shall be binding on the married woman and all persons claiming under her. And all surrenders theretofore made of lands similarly circumstanced, where the wife shall have been separately examined by the person taking the surrender, are thereby declared to be good and valid.

The provisions contained in the 91st section of the act, to which I referred in my last Lecture (*k*), for dispensing with the concurrence of the husband in certain cases, such as lunacy, &c., also extend to surrenders to be made by the wife of lands of any tenure, including of course surrenders of copyholds.

Married woman bare trustee.

The Vendor and Purchaser Act, 1874 (*l*), provides (*m*) that where any copyhold hereditaments shall be vested in a married woman as a bare trustee, she may surrender the same as if she were a *feme sole*.

Customary freeholds.

We have already spoken of customary freeholds (*n*), or lands held by copy of court roll, according to the custom of a manor; but which lands are not expressed to be held at the will of the lord. These customary freeholds are in fact a species of copyhold, and are governed by the same laws. There are, however, such things as freehold lands held in fee simple, or for any other estate known to the law, the seisin of which is in the tenant, and the rights incidental to which are all

(*k*) Ante, p. 114.
(*l*) Stat. 37 & 38 Vict. c. 78.
(*m*) Sect. 6.
(*n*) Ante, p. 49.

the rights incidental to freehold lands, and which in truth are freehold lands; but, at the same time, are subject by custom to some peculiar method of alienation. These lands are sometimes called customary freeholds, an appellation which has caused in some cases great confusion between such lands and those copyhold lands which are usually called customary freeholds. I would rather call these lands freehold lands subject to a customary mode of alienation. The case in Coke's Reports which I mentioned in my first Lecture (*o*) is an example of freehold lands subject to a customary method of alienation. In that case a custom within the manor of Porchester, in the county of Kent, was held good, which made void any feoffment of lands held of the manor, unless the same were presented at a court of the manor, to be held within a certain time after the feoffment was made. In that case it was said that the custom of Lidford Castle, in the county of Devon, is, that the freeholder of inheritance cannot pass his freehold, unless by surrender into the hands of the lord. This custom certainly is a very strange one; and I am not aware of any other instance of the alienation of freeholds in a similar manner. The rule generally adopted is, that, if the mode of conveyance is surrender into the hands of the lord and admission, the lands are copyhold, and not freehold. But, in point of principle, I cannot see why any customary mode of alienation of a freehold estate may not be valid. Anciently lands were not alienable by will; nevertheless, by the custom of London and some other towns, lands might anciently have been conveyed by will. And that there are freeholds, subject to a customary mode of alienation, is the opinion of Lord Coke, Lord Hale, Sir William Blackstone, and Sir John Leach. And in the case of *Busher*, appellant, *Thompson*,

Freehold lands subject to a customary mode of alienation.

(*o*) *Perryman's case*, 5 Rep. 84; ante, p. 11.

respondent (*p*), it was held that a person was entitled to vote as a freeholder in respect of lands situate within the limits of the ancient Borough of Kirby in Kendall, although the burgage tenements had always been conveyed by deed of grant, or bargain and sale, without livery of seisin, and without a lease for a year, or any enrolment. The lease for a year and enrolment will be explained in my next Lecture, in which I hope to treat of alienation by virtue of the Statute of Uses. However, as you see, in this borough freehold lands in possession were capable of being conveyed by deed without any livery of seisin. And the custom was also stated to be that a husband and wife conveyed the burgage tenements of the wife by such deed of grant or bargain and sale as before mentioned, and without any separate examination of the wife. The tenements had also been devisable by will in the same manner as ordinary freehold estates. The Court held that, in the entire absence of anything like base service, it was at liberty to refer the possession of the appellant to a freehold interest, notwithstanding the mode of conveyance was not strictly reconcilable with the common law. There was nothing in the circumstance of the conveyance being by deed, without livery of seisin, that necessarily led to the conclusion that the tenure was base. Mr. Justice Williams observed (*q*) that there might be some difficulty in seeing how the mode of conveyances stated in the case could be operative to pass the estate; but that difficulty would in no degree be lessened by holding the tenements to be of copyhold or base tenure.

Freehold estates subject to a customary mode of alienation may therefore occasionally exist; and when they do exist, they are to be carefully distinguished

(*p*) 4 C. B. 48.

(*q*) Page 62

from what are generally called customary freeholds. For these are lands held by copy of court roll; the tenants of them are at law merely tenants at will, though not expressed to be so, and their only title to the possession of their lands is by virtue of the custom of the manor.

In my next Lecture I hope to speak of the alienation of freehold lands effected by virtue of the Statute of Uses.

LECTURE IX.

Statute of Mortmain.

You may remember that, in a former Lecture, I brought to your notice the Statute of Mortmain, 7th Edward I., stat. 2 (*a*). By this statute, which is also called the *Statutum de Religiosis*, an attempt was made to restrain the ecclesiastics from obtaining lands, which, when in their hands, were said to be in mortmain, and yielded no feudal advantage to the lord, nor any assistance towards the defence of the realm. But the ecclesiastics were not so easily defeated: they obtained feoffments to other persons and their heirs, in trust for, or to the use of, themselves. However, the legislature again interfered; and a statute was passed in the 15th year of King Richard II. (*b*), by which it was agreed and assented, "that all they that be possessed by feoffment or by other manner, *to the use* of religious people or other spiritual persons, of lands, tenements, fees, advowsons or other possessions whatever, to amortise them, and whereof the said religious and spiritual persons do take the profits, that, betwixt this and the feast of St. Michael next coming, they shall *cause them to be amortised by the licence of the king and of the lords, or else that they shall sell and alien them* to some other use between this and the said feast; upon pain to be forfeited to the king and to the lords, according to the form of the said Statute *de Religiosis*, as lands purchased by religious people. And that from thenceforth no such purchase be made, so that such religious or other spiritual persons take thereof the profits as afore is said upon pain aforesaid." And the same statute was also extended to guilds or fraternities, and to

Feoffments to the use of spiritual persons.

(*a*) Ante, pp. 23—25.

(*b*) Stat. 15 Rich. 2, c. 5.

"mayors, bailiffs and commons of cities, boroughs and other towns which have a perpetual commonalty and others which have offices perpetual." The example set by the ecclesiastics was followed in many cases by private persons, who were in the habit of making secret feoffments of lands to their friends, as feoffees to their own use, or to the use of any other person or persons intended to be benefitted. The person to whose use the feoffment was made was called, in Norman French, *cestui que use*. The feoffees were called *feoffees to uses*. The effect of these feoffments was that the real owners of the lands were not known, or, at least, were not easily discovered; contrary to the policy of the law, which required the seisin of lands to be known to the neighbourhood, and when changed to be changed openly. These secret feoffments appear to have caused great trouble and vexation, especially to the purchasers of lands; and, in order to remedy the inconveniences thus occasioned, a statute was passed in the first year of King Richard III. (*c*). This act is intituled "An Act against Privy and Unknown Feoffments." And after reciting the uncertainty and vexations arising from such feoffments, it is enacted, "That every estate, feoffment, gift, release, grant, leases and confirmations of lands, tenements, rents, services or hereditaments, made or had, or hereafter to be made or had, by any person or persons, being of full age, of whole mind, at large, and not in *duress*, to any person or persons, and all recoveries and executions had or made, shall be good and effectual to him to whom it is so made, had or given, and to all other to his use, against the seller, feoffor, donor or grantor thereof, and against the sellers, feoffors, donors or grantors, his and their heirs, claiming the same only as heir or heirs to the same sellers, feoffors, donors or grantors, and every of them, *and against all other having or claiming any title*

Secret feoffments to uses.

Cestui que use.

Feoffment by *cestui que use* good as against feoffees to uses.

(*c*) Stat. 1 Rich. 3, c. 1.

or interest in the same only to the use of the seller, feoffor, donor or grantor, or sellers, feoffors, donors or grantors, or his or their said heirs, at the time of the bargain, sale, covenant, gift or grant made; saving to every person or persons such right, title, action or interest, by reason of any gift in tail thereof made, as they ought to have if this act had not been made."

Effect of statute of 1 Rich. 3, c. 1.

The intention of this statute was to quiet the title of purchasers; so that, if any person took a feoffment from the *cestui que use*, or the person to whose use the lands were held, instead of from the feoffees, to whom the legal seisin had been transferred, he could have a good title as against the feoffees. The *cestui que use* in possession was enabled to make a conveyance, which, by this act, was sufficient to transfer the property, without the concurrence of the feoffees to uses. But the fault of the statute was, that it did not take away from the feoffees to uses the power which they had, as owners of the legal estate, of themselves making a feoffment, and so conveying the lands irrespectively of their *cestui que use*. In fact the feoffees to uses might have made a feoffment to one person by virtue of their estate, and the *cestui que use* might have made a feoffment to another person, by virtue of the power conferred upon him by the statute.

Wardship of heir of *cestui que use*.

One of the effects of conveyances to uses was, that the lords were deprived of the rights to wardships in case the *cestui que use* or beneficial owner, died leaving an infant heir (*d*). This was remedied by a statute of the 4 & 5 Henry VII. (*e*), by which it was provided that the heir of *cestui qui use*, holding his lands by knight's service, being within age, should be in ward, and being of full age should pay relief.

(*d*) Ante, p. 18.

(*e*) Stat. 4 & 5 Hen. 7, c. 17.

Execution against lands held to the use of the debtor.

Another statute of the 19th Henry VII. (*f*), provided that execution should be delivered of all such lands and tenements as any other person or persons were or should be in any manner of wise seised *to the only use of him against whom execution was sued*, like as the sheriff or other officer might or ought to have done, if the party, against whom execution thereafter should be so sued, had been solely seised of such lands and tenements, of such estate as they were seised of to his use at the time of the said execution sued. It was also ordained that the lords of whom any lands were holden in socage, should from thenceforth, after the death of him to whose use any person or persons as is aforesaid were seised, *and no will thereof declared*, have his relief, heriot (*g*), and all other duties, like as the lord ought or might have had if he had died seised of the same. The words "and no will thereof declared" were material, for the use of land was allowed to be disposed of by will; and it was for the sake of the power of making a will that persons often placed their lands in the hands of feoffees to their own use. At this time the legal tenant of lands in fee simple had no power to devise them by his will, except by the custom of gavelkind in Kent and Wales, and by the customs of a few cities and boroughs.

Lords of socage lands to have relief, &c. of *cestui que use*.

Will of *cestui que use*.

Feoffments to trustees for superstitious uses, the uses void.

In the reign of Henry VIII. an act was passed (*h*) which remedied an omission in the Statute of Mortmain. This statute extended only to religious persons and to corporations having perpetual existence. Feoffments to trustees for religious purposes, such as to have *obites* perpetual or the continual service of a priest for ever, were considered to be equally objectionable; and this statute, though it did not make the conveyance itself void, nor give the lord a right to enter, yet made all

(*f*) Stat. 19 Hen. 7, c. 15.

(*g*) A short account of heriots will be found in Appendix A.

(*h*) Stat. 23 Hen. 8, c. 10.

such uses void. The statute, however, was not considered to extend to uses of a charitable kind. The statute, it was said, was made to take away such superstitious uses as to pray for souls supposed to be in Purgatory and the like, and not to forbid the erecting of grammar schools and the relief of poor men (*i*).

The use of lands was held to be descendible according to the rules of the common law, and the use of lands of the tenure of borough English and gavelkind descended according to those customs. The use was also devisable by will, and it was unnecessary that a will should be in writing. The use was alienable, as we have seen; and in the case of a *feme covert* entitled to the use of land, a fine was necessary to enable her to convey her interest. A *cestui que use*, however, had no legal ownership: *that* was vested in the feoffees. The inconveniences arising from the general establishment of uses were considered to be very great; and an attempt was at length made to unite the possession of the lands to the use, so that the *cestui que use* in possession should have not merely an equitable, but a legal estate; and so that the feoffees to uses should be deprived of the estate vested in them by the feoffment, and consequently of all power over the land. This was endeavoured to be effected by a famous act of the 27th of Henry VIII. (*j*), intituled "An Act concerning Uses and Wills," which act is commonly called the Statute of Uses. This statute is still in force, and it is, in fact, the keystone of all modern conveyancing, although, as we shall see, the intent of its framers was in some respects singularly defeated. The first section of the act is as follows:—

Use was descendible.

Statute of Uses.

"Where, by the common laws of this realm, lands, tenements and hereditaments be not devisable by testa-

Sect. 1.

(*i*) *Porter's case*, 1 Rep. 24 a.

(*j*) Stat. 27 Hen. 8, c. 10.

ment, nor ought to be transferred from one to another but by solemn livery and seisin (*k*), matter of record (*l*), writing sufficient made *bonâ fide*, without covin or fraud; yet nevertheless divers and sundry imaginations, subtle inventions and practices have been used, whereby the hereditaments of this realm have been conveyed from one to another by fraudulent feoffments, fines, recoveries and other assurances, craftily made to secret uses, intents and trusts (*m*); and also by wills and testaments (*n*) sometimes made by *nude parolx* and words, sometimes by signs and tokens, and sometimes by writing, and for the most part made by such persons as be visited with sickness, in their extreme agonies and pains, or at such time as they have scantly had any good memory or remembrance; at which times they, being provoked by greedy and covetous persons, lying in wait about them, do many times dispose indiscreetly and unadvisedly their lands and inheritances; by reason whereof, and by occasion of which fraudulent feoffments, fines, recoveries and other like assurances to uses, confidences and trusts, divers and many heirs have been unjustly at sundry times disherited; the lords have lost their wards, marriages, reliefs, harriots, escheats, aids *pur fair chivalier*, and *pur file marier* (*o*), and scantly any person can be certainly assured of any lands by them purchased, nor know surely against whom they shall use their actions or executions (*p*) for their rights, titles and duties; also men married have lost their tenancies by the curtesy, women their dowers, manifest perjuries by trial of such secret wills and uses have been committed; the king's highness hath lost the profits and advantages of the lands of persons attainted, and of the lands craftily put in feoffments to the uses of aliens born, and also the

(*k*) Ante, p. 99.

(*l*) Ante, p. 106.

(*m*) Ante, p. 134.

(*n*) Ante, p. 136.

(*o*) Ante, pp. 18—20. A short account of harriots or heriots will be found in Appendix A.

(*p*) Ante, p. 136.

profits of waste, for a year and a day, of lands of felons attainted, and the lords their escheats thereof; and many other inconveniences have happened, and daily do increase among the king's subjects, to their great trouble and inquietness, and to the utter subversion of the ancient common laws of this realm; for the extirping and extinguishment of all such subtle practised feoffments, fines, recoveries, abuses and errors heretofore used and accustomed in this realm, to the subversion of the good and ancient laws of the same, and to the intent that the king's highness, or any other his subjects of this realm, shall not in any wise hereafter by any means or inventions be deceived, damaged or hurt, by reason of such trusts, uses or confidences: It may please the king's most royal majesty, that it may be enacted by his highness, by the assent of the lords spiritual and temporal, and the commons in this present Parliament assembled, and by the authority of the same, in manner and form following: that is to say, that where any person or persons stand or be seised, or at any time hereafter shall happen to be seised, of and in any honours, castles, manors, lands, tenements, rents, services, reversions, remainders, or other hereditaments, *to the use, confidence or trust* of any other person or persons, or of any body politick, by reason of any bargain, sale, feoffment, fine, recovery, covenant, contract, agreement, will or otherwise, by any manner means whatsoever it be; that in every such case, all and every such person and persons and bodies politick *that have or hereafter shall have any such use, confidence or trust*, in fee simple, fee tail, or term of life or for years, or otherwise, or any use, confidence or trust in remainder or reverter, shall from henceforth stand and be seised, deemed and adjudged *in lawful seisin, estate and possession* of and in the same honours, castles, manors, lands, tenements, rents, services, reversions, remainders and hereditaments, with their appurtenances, *to all intents*, constructions and purposes in the law, of and in *such like estates as they have or shall have in use, trust or confidence* of or in the same; and that *the estate, title, right and possession* that was in such person or persons that were or hereafter shall be seised of any lands, tenements or hereditaments, to the use, confidence or trust of any such person or persons, or of any body politick, be from henceforth clearly *deemed and adjudged to be in him or them that have or hereafter shall have such use, confidence or trust*, after such quality, manner, form and condition as they had before, in or to the use, confidence or trust that was in them."

Sect. 2.

The 2nd section provides for the event of many persons being jointly seised to the use of any of them that are so jointly seised; and it provides that, in every such case, the person or persons *that have or shall have any such use, confidence or trust* in any hereditaments, shall from thenceforth have and be deemed and adjudged to have, *only to him or them*, such estate, possession and seisin in the same hereditaments, in like nature, manner, form, condition and course, as he or they had before in the use, confidence or trust of the same. The act contains other provisions which are not material for our present purpose.

Effect of the Statute of Uses.

The effect of this act was to transfer uses into possession, or to make the person, to whose use lands had been conveyed, himself the legal owner of these lands. The result is, that if, since the passing of this statute, a feoffment is made of lands to A. and his heirs, to the use of B. and his heirs, and the legal seisin of the lands is actually delivered to A., so that he is put into actual possession of the lands, the statute, the very same moment, takes away from him the possession that he had by virtue of the livery of seisin, and vests it in B., the *cestui que use*, for an estate in fee simple. A. is made, as it is said, to be merely a conduit pipe for conveying the fee simple to B. The statute is said to execute the use to B. by turning it into a legal estate. The statute, you will observe, speaks only of persons *seised* of any honours, castles, &c. to the use, confidence or trust of any other person or persons. It does not therefore apply to leaseholds for years; for a leaseholder for years, as we have seen (*q*), though in possession is not seised. Therefore, if land held for a term of years be assigned to A. to the use of B., the statute will not execute this use, but A. will continue in possession for the residue of the term in trust for B. But the statute does speak of persons seised to the use, confidence or trust of persons for term of life or years. Therefore, if A., a person seised in fee, becomes, by any means, seised of land to the use of B. for a term of years, the statute executes this use, and gives B. the actual possession during the term.

The statute executes the use.

Statute does not apply to leaseholds for years.

Statute executes uses for years.

There was one effect of the act that does not appear to have been foreseen by the makers of it, viz. this: If one person became by any "bargain, sale, agreement, or otherwise," seised to the use of another, the other person immediately had vested in him, by the act, the whole possession and seisin of the person who was seised to his use. The consequence of this was that if A., a person seised in fee, sold his land to B., another person, by a mere contract for sale (which at that time might be without any writing), the purchaser was placed, by the contract, in the position of *cestui que use*. The vendor was a person seised to his use, and the result was that, by virtue of the statute, the purchaser instantly had the lawful seisin and possession. A mere verbal contract, therefore, for a pecuniary consideration, and that however small, was sufficient to pass, and did pass, to the purchaser an estate in fee simple in the lands, without any feoffment

Contract for sale.

(*q*) Ante, p. 5.

Enrolment of bargain and and sale.

or livery of seisin. In order to remedy this inconvenience an act of the same session (*r*) was passed, which provides that "no manors, lands, tenements, or other hereditaments, shall pass, alter, or change from one to another, whereby any *estate of inheritance or freehold* shall be made to take effect in any person or persons, or any use thereof to be made, by reason only of any bargain and sale thereof, except the same bargain and sale be made *by writing, indented, sealed, and enrolled* in one of the King's courts of record at Westminster, or else within the same county or counties where the same manors, lands or tenements so bargained and sold lie or be, before the *custos rotulorum* and two justices of the peace and the clerk of the peace of the same county or counties, or two of them at the least, whereof the clerk of the peace to be one; and the same enrolment to be had and made *within six months* next after the date of the same writings indented. But nothing therein contained was to extend to any lands, tenements or hereditaments lying or being within any city, borough or town corporate wherein the mayors, recorders, chamberlains, bailiffs or other officer or officers have authority or have lawfully used to enrol any evidences, deeds or other writings within their precincts. You will observe that the enactment only related to bargains and sales, whereby an *estate of inheritance or freehold* should be made to take effect in any person or persons. The enrolment also was to be made within six months next after the date of the writings indented. A month in law is a lunar month, and not a calendar month, except in mercantile matters, and except also in acts of parliament passed since the fourth of February, 1851 (*s*); so that every bargain and sale must be enrolled within six lunar months from the date.

Six months.

Counties palatine.

A statute of 5 Elizabeth (*t*) made enrolments of deeds

(*r*) Stat. 27 Hen. 8, c. 16.

(*s*) Stat. 13 & 14 Vict. c. 21, s. 4.

(*t*) Stat. 5 Eliz. c. 26.

of bargain and sale of lands in the counties palatine as effectual, if enrolled in the courts of those counties, as they would have been had they been enrolled in any of the Queen's courts at Westminster. And the acts by which registries of deeds were established for the three ridings of the county of York, provided that the enrolment of bargains and sales in those registries shall be as effectual to all intents and purposes as if the same had been enrolled in the Queen's courts under the statute of 27 Henry VIII. These statutes are 5 & 6 Anne, c. 18, s. 1, for the West Riding of the county of York; statute 6 Anne, c. 35, s. 16, for the East Riding and the town and county of the town of Kingston-upon-Hull; and the statute of 8 George II. c. 6, s. 21, for the North Riding of the same county. By the above statutes all copies of enrolments of bargains and sales remaining on record in the registry office are to be allowed, in all courts where such copies shall be produced, to be as good and sufficient as bargains and sales enrolled in any of the courts at Westminster, and the copies of the enrolment thereof. And by a statute of Anne (*u*), it was provided that where any indenture of bargain and sale should be pleaded with a *profert in curiâ*, or offer to produce the same, the person or persons so pleading may produce, by the authority of that act, to answer such *profert, a copy of the enrolment* of such bargain and sale; and such copy, examined with the enrolment, and signed by the proper officer having the custody of such enrolment, and proved upon oath to be a true copy so examined and signed, shall be of the same force and effect to all intents as the indentures of bargain and sale were and should be of, if the same were in such case produced and shown forth.

Yorkshire.

Copies evidence.

A bargain and sale of lands, duly enrolled, is still

Bargain and sale, operation of.

(*u*) Stat. 10 Anne, c. 18, s. 3.

occasionally used. The operation of the instrument is this:—When the bargain and sale is executed, the bargainor becomes seised to the use of the bargainee; and the Statute of Uses immediately transfers to the bargainee the actual seisin and possession of the lands so bargained and sold.

Implied covenants for title.

By virtue of the provisions of the above-mentioned registry acts for Yorkshire and Kingston-upon-Hull, bargains and sales in that county, containing the words *grant, bargain and sell,* imply covenants on the part of the bargainor, for the title to the lands bargained and sold by him, as to his own acts, according to forms set out in the acts (*x*). A pecuniary consideration is absolutely necessary to raise a use, as it is said, by means of a bargain and sale. But any pecuniary consideration, however trifling, is sufficient, such as a payment of five shillings, or the reservation of a rent of twelve pence. And there is no necessity that the money should be actually paid. A bargain and sale is also good, if it be made in consideration of a future payment agreed to be made, as well of a sum stated to be paid at or before the execution of the deed. The proper words in a bargain and sale are the words *bargain and sell;* but these are not absolutely necessary. For a deed of gift, which was intended to operate as a feoffment, was in one case held to be a good bargain and sale, having been enrolled within one month after the making of it, and before any livery of seisin was made. This was decided in an anonymous case, reported in the third volume of Leonard's Reports (*y*).

Consideration.

Words.

Enrolment relates back.

The conveyance effected by a bargain and sale is not perfect until enrolment; but the enrolment is said to relate back to the delivery of the deed, so as to avoid

(*x*) Stat. 6 Anne, c. 35, ss. 30, 34, and 8 Geo. 2, c. 6, s. 35.

(*y*) Page 16.

any mesne or intermediate conveyances, if any should have been made by the bargainor. In some cases, a bargain and sale may operate either as a conveyance at the common law, or by virtue of the Statute of Uses; and in these cases the rule is that, if it can operate as a common law conveyance, it shall do so, unless the bargainee should elect that it shall operate under the statute; but this election must be made by him in his lifetime. Of this rule the case of *Haigh* v. *Jagger* (z) is an instructive example.

Election.

Haigh v. *Jagger*.

The statute which required enrolment only related to bargains and sales for money: it did not touch the raising of a use by means of a covenant entered into by any person to stand seised of his lands to the use of some other person connected with him by blood or marriage. A conveyance of land may therefore be made by means of a *covenant to stand seised*. When a deed is executed by the owner of land, by which he covenants to stand seised of the land to the use of any of his relations, the land itself passes by virtue of the Statute of Uses. The covenantor is deprived, by the statute, of his legal possession; and it is vested, by the same statute, in the covenantee. The covenant, like every other covenant, must be by deed; the consideration of blood or marriage is absolutely necessary. The covenantor must have vested in him an estate of freehold in the lands. But it is not absolutely necessary that the words *covenant to stand seised* should be used. A conveyance in the form of a grant, feoffment or release may take effect as a covenant to stand seised, if there be the consideration of blood or marriage between the parties.

Covenant to stand seised.

Consideration.

Words.

But for many years the ordinary mode of conveyance

(z) 3 Exch. 54.

Lease and release.

was by *lease and release;* the lease operating as a bargain and sale under the statute of uses; the release operating, independently of that statute, as a release to the bargainee by way of enlargement of his estate (*a*). This occurred as follows: It was perceived that, whilst the Statute of Uses applied to all estates, even for years, of which one person was seised to the use of another, the statute which required the enrolment of bargains and sales applied only to the passing of estates of inheritance and freehold. If, therefore, A., a person seised in fee, bargained and sold his lands to B. for a year in consideration of 5*s*., B. was put, by the Statute of Uses, into immediate actual possession of the lands for a year. Now a tenant in actual possession may, as we saw in our last Lecture (*b*), have a release by deed made to him by his landlord, so as to enlarge his estate to a fee simple, if the release be made to him and his heirs. A bargain and sale for a year, followed by a deed of release to the bargainee, his heirs and assigns, was a *lease and release;* and was, until the year 1841, the common mode of conveying lands in this kingdom. It is surprising that persons should have gone on for so many years using two deeds for every conveyance when a very short act of parliament might have rendered one only necessary. But reforms come slowly. In this case Ireland set an example; and by an Irish act (*c*) the recital of the bargain and sale or lease for a year in the release was made evidence that there had been a bargain and sale, though in fact there had not. So that practically a bargain and sale for a year was never executed in Ireland. But in England the waste of parchment still continued, until, in the year 1841, an act was passed (*d*) intituled "An Act for rendering a release as effectual for

Irish enactment.

English enactments.

(*a*) Ante, p. 119.

(*b*) Ante, p. 120.

(*c*) Stat. 9 Geo. 2, c. 5, amended and made perpetual by the Irish act, 1 Geo. 3, c. 3.

(*d*) Stat. 4 & 5 Vict. c. 21.

the conveyance of freehold estates as a lease and release by the same parties." This act enacted that a release which should be executed on or after the 15th of May, 1841, *and should be expressed to be made in pursuance of that act*, should be as effectual for the purposes therein expressed as if the releasing party or parties had executed a deed of bargain and sale, or lease for a year for giving effect to such release, although no such bargain and sale or lease for a year should be executed. The act also contains a beneficial provision (*e*) that the recital in any deed of release, executed before the act, of the lease for a year shall be conclusive evidence of the bargain and sale or lease for a year having been made.

The act to simplify the transfer of property (*f*) was the first to provide directly that any person might convey by any deed, without livery of seisin or a prior lease, all such freehold land as he might, before the passing of the act, have conveyed by lease and release. This act, however, was repealed by an act of the next session of parliament, the Act to amend the Law of Real Property, to which we have before referred. This act (*g*) now enacts (*h*), that after the 1st of October, 1845, all corporeal tenements and hereditaments shall, as regards the conveyance of the immediate freehold thereof, be deemed to lie in grant as well as in livery. This was a somewhat more technical way of saying what the act of the former session had sufficiently said before. But I think you will agree with me that the abolition of two deeds for every conveyance was a very great improvement in the law.

All lands may now be conveyed by grant.

(*e*) Sect. 2.
(*f*) Stat. 7 & 8 Vict. c. 76.
(*g*) Stat. 8 & 9 Vict. c. 106.
(*h*) Sect. 2.

Copyholds.

The Statute of Uses does not apply to copyholds,—for a copyholder has only a quasi seisin (*i*); he is never actually seised, and so cannot be seised to the use of another within the meaning of the Statute of Uses.

In my next Lecture I hope to consider the *seisin of the freehold as it affects settlements.*

(*i*) Ante, p. 42.

LECTURE X.

Settlements.

We now come to the consideration of the seisin of the freehold as it affects the SETTLEMENT of land. And we shall see that the importance which the law attached to the seisin of the freehold, had great influences on the custom of entail, as practised in modern times; giving to the first tenant for life under a settlement, generally the father, an important control over the power of alienation possessed by the tenant in tail in remainder, generally his eldest son, by requiring the concurrence of the owner of the freehold to the proceedings by which the entail and remainders could alone be barred. And we shall see how this control now exists in another shape, by virtue of the office of *protector of the settlement*, which has been created by the act by which fines and recoveries were abolished (*a*). We shall also see that the importance which was attached to the seisin of the freehold anciently prevented the modern mode of settlement, by means of a contingent remainder, after an estate for life in the father, to his eldest unborn son in tail; until means were devised for the preservation of such contingent remainders, by the interposition of an estate vested in trustees for the purpose of preserving them. We shall also see that the rule, which required the seisin of the freehold to be always in some ascertained person, is still in operation, and is, in some cases, one of great hardship, being the means of destroying gifts, which were clearly intended to be for the benefit of persons whom the law yet forbids to take, simply by

Protector.

(*a*) Stat. 3 & 4 Will. 4, c. 74.

reason of the continued existence of an ancient technical rule (*b*).

Estate tail.

In pursuing this subject, it is my intention to speak, first, of estates tail in possession; next, of estates tail in remainder; and, thirdly, of contingent remainders. An estate tail is said to owe its origin to the statute *De donis conditionalibus*, commonly called the statute *De donis* (*c*); also called the Statute of Westminster the 2nd. Before this statute, lands might either have been granted to a man and his heirs, giving him an estate in fee simple, or they might have been granted to a man and the heirs of his body. In this case, the gift was said to be a *conditional gift*, the condition being, that he should have heirs of his body. Before he had issue born, he could only alienate the lands as against his issue, if any. But the moment he had issue born, he was enabled to alienate the lands to any other person for an estate in fee simple; thus depriving both his issue of their expected inheritance, and the donor of his expectancy of the lands reverting to himself or his heirs, in the event of the failure of the issue of the donee. If, however, the donee made no alienation, and died without issue, then the lands reverted to the donor or his heirs.

Conditional gift.

This was felt by the great lords, in the time of Edward I., to be a hardship, inasmuch as, by the alienation of their tenants, to whom lands had been thus given, they lost the chance of again possessing the lands in the event of the failure of the issue of the donee. It was in order to remedy this grievance that they procured the passing of the statute *De donis* (*c*). This statute enacts as follows: "First, concerning lands

Statute *De donis*.

(*b*) I am happy to say that this hardship has now been abolished, by stat. 40 & 41 Vict. c. 33, (passed since these Lectures were delivered), a copy of which, with some remarks thereon, will be found in Appendix B.

(*c*) Stat. 13 Edw. 1, c. 1.

that many times are given upon condition, that is to wit, where any giveth his land to any man and his wife and to the heirs begotten of the bodies of the same man and his wife, with such condition expressed that, if the same man and his wife die without heirs of their bodies between them begotten, the land so given shall revert to the giver or his heir. In case also where one giveth lands in free marriage, which gift hath a condition annexed, though it be not expressed in the deed or gift, which is this, that if the husband and wife die without heir of their bodies begotten, the land so given shall revert to the giver or his heir. In case also where one giveth land to another and the heirs of his body issuing, it seemed very hard, and yet seemeth, to the givers and their heirs, that their will being expressed in the gift was not heretofore, nor yet is, observed. For in all the cases aforesaid, after issue begotten and born, between them to whom the lands were given under such condition, heretofore such feoffees had power to alien the land so given, and to disinherit their issue of the land, contrary to the minds of the givers, and contrary to the form expressed in the gift. And further, whereas, by default of issue of such feoffees, the lands so given ought to return to the giver or his heir, by form expressed in the deed of gift, though the issue, if any were, had died. Yet, by the deed and feoffment of them to whom land was so given upon condition, the donors have heretofore been barred of their reversion of such lands, which was directly repugnant to the form of the gift. Wherefore our lord the King, perceiving how necessary and expedient it is to provide remedy in the aforesaid cases, hath ordained that the will of the giver, according to the form in the deed of gift manifestly expressed, shall be from henceforth observed; so that they to whom the land was so given under condition, shall not have power to alien the land so given, whereby it shall fail to remain unto the issue of them

Frank marriage.

Gift in tail.

Will of the giver to be observed.

to whom it was given, after their death, or shall revert unto the giver or his heir, if issue fail, either for that there is no issue at all, or if there be any issue, it fail by death, the heir of the body of such issue failing."

This statute points to the two methods of settling lands which were in existence at the time of the passing of the statute, and continued long afterwards to be the usual methods of settling lands in England:—methods, however, which became obsolete about the time of the Commonwealth, in consequence of other devices for the settling of lands being resorted to by conveyancers. One of these ancient methods was, as the statute says, where one giveth lands in *free marriage*, or *frank marriage* as it was more usually called; which gift, says the statute, hath a condition annexed, though it be not expressed in the deed of gift, which is this; that, if the husband and wife die without heir of their bodies begotten, the land so given shall revert to the giver or his heir. This is adverted to by Littleton; who, in his 17th section has these words, "In the same manner it is, where tenements are given by one man to another with a wife, which is the daughter or cousin to the giver, in *frank marriage*, the which gift hath an inheritance by these words *frank marriage* annexed unto it, although it be not expressly said or rehearsed in the gift, that is to say, that the donees shall have the tenements to them and to their heirs between them two begotten. And this is called especial tail because the issue of the second wife may not inherit." Littleton adds (*e*), "In every gift in tail, without more saying, the reversion of the fee simple is in the donor. And the donees and their issue shall do to the donor and to his heirs the like services as the donor doth to his lord next paramount; except the donees in frank marriage who shall hold

Frank marriage.

(*e*) Sect. 19.

quietly from all manner of service (unless it be for fealty), until the fourth degree is past; and after the fourth degree is past, the issue in the fifth degree, and so forth the other issues after him, shall hold of the donor or of his heirs as they hold over, as before is said." The holding free from all manner of service for four generations was a great advantage in the case of a gift in frank marriage. Such gifts are now, however, quite obsolete, as are also the other gifts mentioned in the statute, namely, gifts to a man and his wife and to the heirs begotten of the bodies of the same man and his wife. This gift, which created, before the statute, a fee simple conditional, after the statute created an estate which was called an estate in special tail; whilst a simple gift, when it occurred, to a man and the heirs of his body, created an estate which was called an estate tail. Littleton says (*f*), "Note that this word *talliare* is the same as to set to some certainty, or to limit to some certain inheritance. And for that it is limited and put in certain what issue shall inherit by force of such gifts, and how long the inheritance shall endure, it is called in Latin *feodum talliatum*, i. e. *hæreditas in quandam certitudinem limitata*. For, if a tenant in general tail dieth without issue, the donor or his heirs may enter as in their reversion."

Gift to a man and his wife and the heirs of their bodies.

Special tail.

Estate tail.

The effect of the statute *De donis* was, as you see, to prevent the husband and the wife from alienating the land, so as that it should fail to remain to their issue after their death, or so that it should fail to revert unto the giver or his heirs, if their issue should fail, either by reason of there being no issue at all, or by reason of the subsequent failure of the issue at any future time. After the passing of this statute therefore land that was entailed, that is, land which was

Effect of the statute *De donis*.

(*f*) Sect. 18.

either given in frank marriage, or settled on a man and his wife and the heirs of their bodies, or settled simply upon a man and the heirs of his body, still continued to devolve to the next heir mentioned in the gift *per formam doni*, according to the form of the gift, from generation to generation, descending from the last heir of the body of the donee, to the next heir of his body, according to the rules of descent, and so on, for so long a time as any issue of his body continued in existence. At the end of which time, however remote that time might have been, the estate tail ceased, and the land again reverted to the donor or his heirs. The donor and his heirs, therefore, by virtue of this statute, had a reversion in fee simple in the lands entailed, which reversion was vested in him and them, and came into possession on the extinction of the issue of the tenant in tail.

Taltarum's case.

The way in which this statute was defeated is a tale that has been often told. This enactment of the Legislature was in fact set aside by a decision of the courts of law, in a famous case called *Taltarum's case*, which occurred in the twelfth year of the reign of King Edward IV. It is reported in the Year Book, twelfth of Edward IV. (*g*). You will find a translation of the report, which in the original is in Norman-French, at p. 182 of a valuable work lately published by Mr. Kenelm Edward Digby, being an introduction to the History of the Law of Real Property, with original authorities. In this case the court sanctioned a *feigned recovery* of the lands by action at law as a bar to the issue in tail, and also to the reversioner; thus enabling a tenant in tail to do more than he could have done before the statute *De donis*. For before the statute *De donis* he could not alien as against the

Feigned recovery.

(*g*) Page 19.

donor or his heirs until he had issue born; but by virtue of the law as created by the judges, and as afterwards well established, a tenant in tail, the moment after the gift, could sell the lands for an estate in fee simple, and so entirely defeat both his own issue and also the reversioner, to whom the land was limited in default of his issue.

Ancient actions for lands.

In order to the better understanding of this case, it is desirable to say a few words with respect to the actions for recovering lands which existed in ancient times; all which actions, however, were abolished by the statute of 3 & 4 Will. 4, c. 27, the present statute of limitation. At the present time there is but one action for the recovery of land; and that is, an action of *ejectment*, which tries not necessarily the right to the legal seisin, but simply the right to the *possession* of the lands. The ancient law made a distinction between a right of entry and a right of action. If a person were disseised, he had a right of entry, which he might exercise by entering in a peaceable manner, and not with force or with a strong hand. If his entry were forbidden, he might then make his claim, going as near as he dare (*h*), or he might bring his action. If the disseisor died whilst in possession, leaving an heir, the right of entry of the disseisee was lost, and he was driven to his action (*i*). But by a statute of Henry VIII. (*k*), the descent of the lands to the heir of the disseisor did not take away the disseisee's right of entry, unless the disseisor had had the peaceable possession of the lands by the space of five years next after the disseisin. Actions for the recovery of land were called real actions, because the real land itself was recovered; and it was necessary for the demandant to allege and prove a *seisin* of the tenements in question, either in his own person, or in that of some

Ejectment.

Rights of entry and actions.

(*h*) Ante, pp. 3, 100.

(*i*) Ante, p. 102.

(*k*) Stat. 32 Hen. 8, c. 33.

Real actions possessory and droitural.

other person, under whom he claimed. Real actions were divided into *actions possessory* and *actions droitural;* the former trying the right to the feudal possession or seisin, and the latter—which were considered the highest kind of action—trying the right of property to the entire fee simple. The foundation of the droitural ac-

Writ of right.

tion was a *writ of right;* and it was usually resorted to only in cases where a possessory action could no longer

Writs of entry.

be brought. The foundations of possessory actions were writs called *writs of entry*, framed to meet the circumstances of each class of cases. The writ was called,

Præcipe quod reddat.

from its first words, *præcipe quod reddat.* It was directed to the sheriff, and required him to *command so and so* (the tenant seised of the land) *that he give up* to the demandant, without delay, so much land in such a vill which the demandant claimed to be his right and inheritance, &c. This writ was obliged to be brought against the person who was *seised of the freehold*, and could not be brought against any other person.

Warranty.

We have seen that in many cases, where lands were given, there was an express warranty of the title to the lands made by the feoffor; and that, in default of express warranty, the receipt of homage from the feoffee implied a warranty, as did also the word *give* used in a feoffment (*l*). The doctrine of warranty was somewhat complicated, and happily it now forms no part of our law. But it is necessary to speak of it in order to understand the bar of an estate tail and remainder over. In the case of an attempt to recover lands by a real action, the first step taken by the tenant was usually the vouching or calling to warranty of the person who had warranted the title. In case of eviction of the donee from the lands given to him, the donor was bound, by his warranty, to give him lands of equal

(*l*) Ante, pp. 101, 102.

value. When, therefore, lands given to a man and the heirs of his body had been warranted by the donor, if the donee were evicted, the donor was bound to substitute other lands to be settled in like manner. This afforded the means of barring an estate tail by means of a fictitious warranty. The tenant in tail procured a friend to bring against him a collusive action by means of a writ of entry; the tenant vouched to warranty some other person, who acknowledged that he had warranted the title to the lands, after which he took the place of the tenant, and, instead of defending the action, he allowed judgment to go against himself by default. In later times, the person who undertook to warrant everybody's lands was the crier of the Court, who, of course, had no lands to give in return; nevertheless judgment was had under the writ that the demandant should recover the lands in question, and so he became seised of them to himself and his heirs. The tenant in tail had also judgment to recover a recompense of lands of equal value against the defaulter, which, of course, he never did, because the defaulter had no lands to give, and by this means the estate tail was said to be barred and turned into an estate in fee simple. I have given a short account of the proceedings in these Common Recoveries, as they were called, in the chapter on estates tail in my Principles of the Law of Real Property (*m*); and as the time when recoveries were used as common modes of assurance is getting every year more distant, I think it hardly desirable that I should go further into them.

Common Recoveries.

It became in time a maxim of law, that every tenant in tail in possession had a right to bar his estate tail, and the remainders over, if any, together with the reversion in fee, by what was called suffering a common

(*m*) Pages 46, 47, 12th ed.

recovery. And any device to prevent him from suffering a recovery, such as a gift to him and the heirs of his body, on the express condition that he should suffer no recovery, was, notwithstanding the statute *De donis*, afterwards held to be fruitless and void, and contrary to the policy of the law.

Mary Portington's case.

Thus in *Mary Portington's case* (*n*) lands were devised by will to several sisters successively in tail, with a proviso that if any of them should conclude and agree to or for the doing or executing of any act, whereby the lands in tail, or any estate or remainder thereof, should by any means be discontinued or aliened, or should do any act or thing whereby the lands might not descend, remain or come, as limited by the will, then the person so concluding and agreeing to or for the doing or executing of any such act should, immediately after such conclusion and agreement, lose and forfeit such estate and benefit as she and they might claim, in such manner as if she or they had never been named in the will; and thenceforth the estate limited to her or them should utterly cease, as fully to all intents and purposes as if she or they were dead without heirs of their bodies. The first tenant in tail agreed to suffer a common recovery, and suffered one accordingly. The next person in remainder claimed the estate as forfeited; but it was adjudged that a tenant in tail cannot be restrained by any condition or limitation from suffering a recovery, and that the clause of forfeiture was void.

Fine.

A tenant in tail in possession might also have discontinued the estate tail, as it was called (*o*), by levying a fine. The statute of the 4th & 5th of Henry VII., c. 24, to which I adverted in a former Lecture (*p*), and

(*n*) 10 Co. Rep. 36. See also *Dawkins* v. *Lord Penrhyn*, L. R., 6 Ch. Div. 318.

(*o*) Ante, p. 103.

(*p*) Ante, p. 109.

which regulated the levying of fines with proclamation, was held to bar the issue in tail after five years' non-claim by them. And this was soon followed by a statute of the 32nd year of Henry VIII. (*q*), by which it was provided, that all fines " with proclamations according to the said statute, by any person or persons of the full age of twenty-one years, of any manors, lands, tenements, or hereditaments, before the time of the said fine levied in any wise entailed to the person or persons so levying the same fine, or to any the ancestor or ancestors of the same person or persons in possession, reversion, remainder or in use, shall be, immediately after the same fine levied, engrossed and proclamations made, adjudged, accepted, deemed and taken to all intents and purposes a sufficient bar and discharge for ever, *against the said person and persons and their heirs, claiming the same lands, tenements and hereditaments, or any parcel thereof, only by force of any such entail*, and against all other persons claiming the same or any parcel thereof only to their use, or to the use of any manner of heir of the bodies of them; any ambiguity, doubt, or contrariosity of opinion risen or grown upon the said estatute to the contrary notwithstanding." By virtue of this act a fine levied by a tenant in tail in possession operated as a bar to his issue. It also discontinued the remainder or reversion in fee, and turned it to a right, to be enforced in a real action by a writ called a writ of formedon in the remainder or formedon in the reverter; which writ being now abolished, it cannot be enforced at all.

There were certain exceptions to the right, which the law gave to every tenant in tail in possession to acquire the clear fee simple by suffering a recovery, or to bar the issue in tail by levying a fine. One of these was the case of a *tenant in tail after the possibility of issue* Tenant in tail after pos-

(*q*) Stat. 32 Hen. 8, c. 36.

sibility of issue extinct.

extinct; that is, where lands were given to a man and his wife and the heirs of their bodies, and one of them died without issue. The survivor became tenant in tail after possibility of issue extinct; for the possibility of any issue inheriting was extinct. The issue of such person by a second marriage could not inherit the estate tail. An act of the reign of Queen Elizabeth (*r*) prohibited recoveries from being suffered by any tenant in tail after possibility of issue extinct. The same act also prohibited recoveries from being suffered by persons who were only tenants for life, or for estates determinable on any life or lives, unless made with the assent of the person or persons to whom any reversion or remainder of the lands then should or ought to appertain. Another exception was, when a woman was tenant in tail of lands settled on her by her husband, or tenant in tail *ex provisione viri*. Such a tenant in tail was prohibited by a statute of Henry VII. (*s*) from suffering a recovery of the lands in tail, without the assent recorded or enrolled of the persons entitled in remainder. She was also prohibited from levying a fine by the 2nd section of the statute 32 of Henry VIII., c. 36, to which I have just referred (*t*). Another exception to the right to suffer a recovery or levy a fine occurred in the case of a tenant in tail, under a grant from the Crown as a reward for public services, whilst the reversion continued in the Crown. This restriction was imposed by an act of the 34 & 35 of Henry VIII. (*u*), intituled "An Act to embar feigned recovery of lands wherein the King's Majesty is in reversion." This act does not extend to estates tail granted by the Crown for other considerations than as a reward for public services. This was decided in the case of *the*

Tenants for life.

Tenant in tail *ex provisione viri*.

Grantee of the Crown for public services.

(*r*) Stat. 14 Eliz., c. 8.
(*s*) Stat. 11 Hen. 7, c. 20.
(*t*) Ante, p. 159.
(*u*) Stat. 34 & 35 Hen. 8, c. 20.

Duke of Grafton v. *London and Birmingham Railway Company* (x).

Act for the abolition of fines and recoveries.

Thus the law continued until the year 1833, when the act was passed for the abolition of fines and recoveries and for the substitution of more simple modes of assurance (y). This act abolished all fines and recoveries after the 31st December, 1833; and also rendered (z) all warranties of lands, made after that date by any tenant in tail thereof, absolutely void against the issue in tail, and all persons whose estates are to take effect after the determination or in defeasance of the estate tail. It then gives (a) full power to "every actual tenant in tail, whether in possession, remainder, contingency, or otherwise, after the 31st of December, 1833, to dispose of, for an estate in fee simple absolute, or for any less estate, the lands entailed, as against all persons claiming the lands entailed by force of any estate tail, which shall be vested in or might be claimed by, or which, but for some previous act, would have been vested in or might have been claimed by, the person making the disposition, at the time of his making the same, and also as against all persons, including the king's most excellent majesty, his heirs and successors, whose estates are to take effect after the determination or in defeasance of any such estate tail; saving always the rights of all persons in respect of estates prior to the estate tail, in respect of which such disposition shall be made, and the rights of all other persons, except those against whom such disposition is by this act authorized to be made."

Warranties now void against issue in tail and remainders and reversion.

Power for tenant in tail to dispose of fee simple.

Exceptions.

The act then provides (b) that where, under any settlement made before the passing of the act, any woman shall be tenant in tail of lands within the provisions of the act of 11 Henry VII., c. 20, before referred to, that is

(x) 5 Bing. N. C. 27.
(y) Stat. 3 & 4 Will. 4, c. 74.
(z) Sect. 14.
(a) Sect. 15.
(b) Sect. 16.

ex provisione viri (*c*), the power of disposition thereinbefore contained as to such lands shall not be exercised by her, except with such assent as, if the act had not been passed, would, under the provisions of the act of Henry VII., have rendered valid a fine or common recovery levied or suffered by her of such lands. But the act provides (*d*) that, except as to lands comprised in any settlement made before the passing of the act, the said act of the 11 Henry VII. shall be and the same is thereby repealed. The statute also provides (*e*) that the power of disposition thereinbefore contained shall not extend to tenants of estates tail who, by the act above referred to (*f*) of the 34 & 35 Henry VIII., intituled "An Act to embar feigned Recovery of Lands wherein the King is in Reversion," or by any other act, are restrained from barring their estates tail, or to tenants in tail after possibility of issue extinct.

Disposition of estate in fee an absolute bar.

The act then contains a provision (*g*) respecting a disposition by the tenant in tail of an estate in fee by way of mortgage, or for any other limited purpose; and such a disposition is made an absolute bar, in equity as well as at law, to all persons as against whom such disposition is by the act authorized to be made, notwithstanding any intention expressed to the contrary. But if the estate created by the disposition is only an estate *pur autre vie*, or for years, absolute or determinable, or if any interest, charge, lien or incumbrance is created, without a term of years absolute or determinable, or any greater estate for securing or raising the same, then such disposition is to be in equity a bar only as far as may be necessary to give full effect to the mortgage or such other limited purpose, or to such interest,

Disposition of less estate a partial bar.

(*c*) Ante, p. 160.
(*d*) Sect. 17.
(*e*) Sect. 18.
(*f*) Ante, p. 160.
(*g*) Sect. 21.

lien, charge or incumbrance, notwithstanding any expression of any intention to the contrary.

The act further enacts (*h*), that every disposition of lands under the act by a tenant in tail thereof shall be effected by some one of the assurances, not being a will, by which such tenant in tail could have made the disposition, if his estate were an estate at law in fee simple absolute. Provided, nevertheless, that no disposition by a tenant in tail shall be of any force, either at law or in equity under the act, unless made or evidenced by deed, and that no disposition by a tenant in tail resting only in contract, either express or implied or otherwise, and whether supported by a valuable or meritorious consideration or not, shall be of any force at law or in equity under the act, notwithstanding such disposition shall be made or evidenced by deed. And if the tenant in tail making the disposition shall be a married woman, the concurrence of her husband shall be necessary to give effect to the same; and any deed which may be executed by her for effecting the disposition shall be acknowledged by her as therein directed. I have already referred to the provisions of the act respecting the acknowledgments of deeds by married women (*i*). It has been held, that the acknowledgment may be made after the enrolment in the Court of Chancery, required by the section I am about to mention (*k*).

Deed required.

Contract insufficient.

Married woman.

The act further provides (*l*), that no assurance by which any disposition of lands shall be effected under the act by a tenant in tail thereof (except a lease for any term not exceeding twenty-one years to commence from the date of such lease, or from any time not

(*h*) Sect. 40.

(*i*) Ante, p. 112.

(*k*) *In re London Dock Act, ex parte Taverner*, 20 Beav. 490; affirmed, 7 De Gex, Macn. & Gordon, 627.

(*l*) Sect. 41.

exceeding twelve calendar months from the date of such lease, where a rent shall be thereby reserved, which, at the time of granting such lease, shall be a rack rent, or not less than five-sixth parts of a rack rent) shall have any operation under the act, unless it be *enrolled in his Majesty's High Court of Chancery* (now represented by the Chancery Division of the High Court) *within six calendar months* after the execution thereof; and if the assurance by which any disposition of lands shall be effected under the act, shall be a bargain and sale, such assurance, although not enrolled within the time prescribed by the act of the 27th of Henry VIII. for enrolment of bargains and sales (which, you may remember, was six *lunar* months (*m*)), shall, if enrolled in the said Court of Chancery within the time prescribed by that clause, be as good and valid as the same would have been, if the same had been enrolled in the said Court within the time prescribed by the act of Henry VIII.

Deed to be enrolled.

The result.

The result is, that a tenant in tail in possession may now grant a binding lease for twenty-one years, at the rent above mentioned, without any enrolment; and he may alien the lands entailed for an estate in fee simple, or any less estate, by any assurance by which a tenant in fee simple can alienate his estate. And such alienation will be good, both as against the tenant in tail, and all the issue in tail, and all remainders and reversions expectant on the failure of such issue, provided the deed be enrolled in the Chancery Division of the High Court of Justice (now substituted for the Court of Chancery), within six calendar months next after the execution thereof.

Copyholds. Where no custom to entail.

The entail of copyholds depends upon the custom of the manor. In some manors there is no custom to en-

(*m*) Ante, p. 142.

tail copyholds; and in these manors a surrender to the use of A. and the heirs of his body gives him a conditional customary fee, corresponding to the conditional fee which was created in freehold lands by a similar gift, prior to the passing of the statute *De donis* (n). Before he has issue he cannot alien, except so far as to bind his issue; after he has had issue, he may alien for a customary estate in fee simple. In some manors estates tail are allowed by the custom; and in these manors, according to the ordinary custom, an estate tail was formerly barrable by a simple surrender; although in some manors a *customary recovery* was required to be suffered in the lord's court; and in other manors, the entail was destroyed by a collusive *forfeiture* of the lands into the hands of the lord, and a *re-grant* of them by him for a customary estate in fee. By the 50th section of the Act for Abolishing Fines and Recoveries, all the previous clauses in the act are rendered applicable to lands held by copy of court roll, so far as circumstances and the different tenures will admit. Copyhold estates tail are to be barred by surrender, if estates at law; but if merely estates in equity, they may be barred either by surrender or by deed. No enrolment in the Chancery Division is required in the case of copyholds. But all the proceedings are entered on the court rolls of the manor; and if a tenant in tail of copyhold lands, whose estate is merely one in equity, should make a disposition by deed, it has been decided that it must be entered on the court rolls within six calendar months from its date (o). In this, as in other cases, the law of copyholds is analogous to the law of freeholds; though at the same time it is sufficiently distinct to require a separate study.

Custom to entail.

Surrender.

Customary recovery.

Forfeiture and re-grant.

Copyhold estates tail at law now barred by surrender.

Entry on court rolls.

There is yet another kind of estate tail, of which it

(n) Ante, p. 150.

(o) *Gibbons* v. *Snape*, 32 Beav. 130.

Quasi entail. may be desirable to say a few words; this is a *quasi entail* of estates held *pur autre vie.* Lands held for the life of A. may be given to B. and his heirs, or to B. and the heirs of his body. If lands so held are given to B. and his heirs, and B. should die in the lifetime of A., he may dispose of them for the residue of A.'s life, either by deed or by his will. The power of testamentary disposition in this case was given to him by the Statute of Frauds (*p*), and in more recent times by the act for the amendment of the laws with respect to wills, commonly called the Wills Act (*q*). But if the gift be to B. and the heirs of his body, what is called a *quasi entail* is created. The gift is not considered as creating an estate analogous to the fee simple conditional at the common law (*r*); but as creating an estate analogous to an estate given to a man and the heirs of his body by a tenant in fee simple, since the passing of the statute *De donis* (*s*). B. cannot, therefore, in this case dispose by will of his interest in the lands, should A. survive him. But, on the other hand, he had no occasion, in order to bar the heir of his body, to do any act analogous to suffering a common recovery or levying a fine. He was able to bar his quasi entail, and all remainders thereon, if any, by a simple deed of conveyance *inter vivos* (*t*); and the Act for the Abolition of Fines and Recoveries, and for the substitution of more simple modes of assurance (*u*), did not touch this case. So that now B. may effectually bar his quasi estate tail and all remainders thereon by a simple deed of grant; and there is no occasion to enrol the deed in the Chancery Division of the High Court. Should B. die in the lifetime of A. without having thus disposed of his estate,

(*p*) Stat. 29 Car. 2, c. 3, s. 12.

(*q*) Stat. 7 Will. 4 & 1 Vict. c. 26, s. 3.

(*r*) Ante, p. 150.

(*s*) Stat. 13 Edw. 1, c. 6; ante, p. 153.

(*t*) *Allen* v. *Allen*, 2 Dru. & War. 307.

(*u*) Stat. 3 & 4 Will. 4, c. 74.

the heir of his body will come in as a *special occupant*, or a person specially pointed out by the deed of gift to occupy the premises during the residue of the life of A.

Special occupant.

Renewable leaseholds for lives.

Lands held *pur autre vie*, or leaseholds for lives as they are generally called, are often renewable, either by express covenant or by favour of the landlord, on certain terms, so as to continue for ever, fresh lives being constantly substituted, as the old ones drop off. It is abundantly evident that there can be no estate at law in the benefit of a mere covenant to renew a lease. But in equity it is otherwise; and a man who has a lease for lives with a covenant for perpetual renewal is looked upon in equity as having an estate, not only during the existing lives, but also during all possible future lives, which he may deal with as he pleases. He may give this estate to B. and the heirs of his body. Should he do so, B. will have in equity a *quasi estate tail*, which, with any remainders and the reversion thereon, he may bar by deed *inter vivos*, without any enrolment, though not by will. The continuation, so to speak, of his estate, by virtue of the covenant for or the expectation of renewal, follows the disposition of his actual estate for the life or lives actually subsisting.

Copyholds for lives.

By the customs of some manors copyhold estates of inheritance are not allowed. The tenants hold only for a life or lives, either solely, or concurrently, or in remainder one after the other. And there may exist a right of renewal, or there may be merely a hope or expectation of renewal by favour of the lord (*x*). In these cases, therefore, the question, whether or not there is any custom to entail, evidently has no place. This question can only arise where estates of inheritance are permitted by the custom. And, where they are permitted, a gift

(*x*) Ante, p. 42.

to a man and the heirs of his body creates either a customary conditional fee, or a customary estate tail, according as there may not, or as there may, be a custom to entail. But, where the custom allows of life estates only, the law, as to customary estates *pur autre vie* given to a man and the heirs of his body, and equity, as to the right or expectation of renewal of such customary estates given in the same way, follow the analogy of freehold estates limited in the same manner (*y*). A customary *quasi estate tail* is held to be created, which, with the remainders and reversion, the owner thereof may bar by a simple surrender *inter vivos;* but not by a surrender to the use of his will, nor by will without such surrender. And, in default of such a bar, the common law heir of the body of the donee will come in as *special occupant*, exactly as in the case of freehold estates *pur autre vie* limited in a similar manner.

Customary quasi estate tail.

In my next Lecture I hope to consider estates tail in remainder expectant on an estate of freehold.

(*y*) *Edwards* v. *Champion*, 3 De Gex, M. & G. 202.

LECTURE XI.

WE now come to the consideration of an estate tail in remainder expectant on an estate of freehold; as, for example, in the case of lands being given to A. for his life, and after his decease to B. and the heirs of his body. In this case the legal seisin or possession of the lands is in A., the tenant for life; and B., though said, for the want of a better word, to be *seised*, has not the legal seisin, but has only an estate of an incorporeal nature so long as A., the tenant for life, is living—or, rather, so long as his estate endures (*a*).

An estate tail in remainder expectant on an estate of freehold.

Now B. in this case may, if he pleases, wait until the decease of A. He will then have a seisin in law before entry, and, after he has entered, he will have a seisin in deed; and, being so seised, he might, in former times, have suffered a common recovery and acquired the fee simple. If any stranger should wrongfully get possession before him, or *intrude*, as it is called, he must have entered on the intruder before he could have had seisin of the lands. A wrongful entry against a remainderman or reversioner is called an *intrusion;* whilst, as we have seen (*b*), a wrongful entry against an heir is called an *abatement*. But during the life of A., the tenant for life, B. alone could not suffer a recovery. I mentioned in my last Lecture that a writ of entry for suffering a common recovery could only be brought against the person who had the legal seisin of the lands (*c*). The consequence was, that a tenant in tail in remainder expectant on an estate of freehold, was

Recovery after death of tenant for life.

Intrusion.

Recovery in lifetime of tenant for life.

(*a*) Ante, pp. 67, 68.
(*b*) Ante, p. 54.
(*c*) Ante, p. 156.

unable to suffer a recovery without the concurrence of the tenant for life or other freeholder. The tenant for life must either have had the writ issued against himself, or he must have conveyed his life estate to some other person for that purpose. This was the course usually pursued. The tenant for life conveyed his estate to a third person, who was called the *tenant to the præcipe* or writ. The tenant to the writ vouched to warranty the tenant in tail, and the tenant in tail vouched over the common vouchee (*d*).

Tenant to the præcipe.

I have said that if the tenant to the *præcipe* had not the freehold, or in other words the actual legal seisin, a common recovery could not be suffered. This rule operated practically in a beneficial manner. In modern times it has been customary to settle lands on the father for his life, with remainder to his eldest son in tail, with remainders over in tail to the other sons; and, by reason of the rule which I have just mentioned, the son could not suffer a recovery, so as to bar the remainders expectant on his estate tail, without the concurrence of his father, the tenant for life, who had the freehold. But with his father's concurrence he was able to do so. In process of time, common recoveries were not only encouraged by the judges, but they were expressly sanctioned by parliament. In some instances, landowners were in the habit of letting their lands to tenants by leases for lives at rents (*e*). These tenants, therefore, had the legal seisin vested in themselves; but there was no object in giving them power to prevent their landlord and his eldest son from suffering a common recovery, by refusing to concur. It was therefore provided by a statute of the reign of King George II. (*f*), that common recoveries suffered, without the surrender of

Concurrence of father tenant for life.

Leaseholds for lives.

Recoveries valid without concurrence

(*d*) Principles of the Law of Real Property, p. 47, 12th ed.

(*e*) Ante, pp. 166, 167.

(*f*) Stat. 14 Geo. 2, c. 20, s. 1.

leases for lives, granted at rents thereby reserved, or without the concurrence of, or any conveyance or assurance from, the lessees, in order to make good tenants to the writs of entry or other writs whereon the recoveries had been or should be suffered, should be valid and effectual in law, to all intents and purposes, as if such lessees had joined in conveying a good estate of freehold, to such persons as had or should become tenants to such writs. It was also provided (*g*), that recoveries should be valid, although the conveyance to the tenant to the writ should be made after the time of the judgment given on the recovery, and the award of the writ of seisin thereupon; provided the same appeared to be made before the end of the term in which the recovery was suffered. Recoveries could only be suffered during term. And this section made a recovery good, though suffered by a person not actually seised, provided he became so before the term was over. The same statute also provided (*h*), that after twenty years from the time of suffering a common recovery, it should be deemed valid to all intents and purposes, notwithstanding the loss of the deed for making the tenant to the writ of entry, if it appear on the face of the recovery that there was a tenant to the writ, and if the persons joining therein had a sufficient estate and power to suffer the same. And the statute also provides (*i*), that after twenty years, where a recovery is necessary to be suffered to complete the title of a purchaser, and there has been possession accordingly, the production of the deeds making the tenant to the writ of entry and declaring the uses of the recovery shall be sufficient evidence for such purchasers, and all claiming under them, that the recoveries were duly suffered, although no record shall appear.

of lessees for lives.

Recoveries valid if conveyance to tenant to writ made in same term.

Loss of deed making tenant to writ.

Protection of purchasers after twenty years.

(*g*) Sect. 6.
(*h*) Sect. 5.
(*i*) Sect. 4.

Remedies for errors in recoveries and fines.

The Act for the Abolition of Fines and Recoveries (*k*) also contains several valuable provisions for the remedying of errors which not unfrequently occurred in the complicated proceedings required for the purpose of levying fines and suffering recoveries. These provisions are contained in sects. 3 to 13 of the act.

Fine by tenant in tail in remainder.

Although a tenant in tail in remainder expectant on an estate for life was unable to suffer a recovery without the concurrence of the tenant for life, he had power, by virtue of the act of the reign of Henry VIII., which I mentioned in my last Lecture (*l*), to bar his own issue by levying a fine. Such a fine, however, unlike a fine levied by a tenant in tail in possession (*m*), had no effect whatever on the remainders or reversion expectant on the determination of the estate tail. For, by such a fine, the seisin, which was in the tenant for life, was not affected; and the result, therefore, of a fine, levied by a tenant in tail in remainder expectant on a life estate, was simply this—that he, by such fine, conveyed the lands to the cognisee and his heirs so long as he, the cognisor of the fine, had issue of his body. An estate to a man and his heirs, so long as he or another has issue of his body, is called a *base fee;* and such a fee a tenant in tail in remainder expectant on an estate of freehold, might have created by levying a fine without requiring the concurrence of the tenant for life. If it should have happened that the immediate remainder or reversion in fee belonged, as might have been the case, to the tenant in tail in remainder himself, then the base fee, if vested in him, would *merge* or be drowned in the immediate remainder or reversion in fee so vested in himself. And, in this way he might acquire a good estate in fee simple in remainder expectant on the decease of the tenant for life.

Base fee.

Merger of base fee.

(*k*) Stat. 3 & 4 Will. 4, c. 74.

(*l*) Stat. 32 Hen. 8, c. 36, s. 1; ante, p. 159.

(*m*) Ante, p. 159.

Thus the law stood until the abolition of fines and recoveries by the act 3 & 4 Will. 4, c. 74. This act, as we have seen (*n*), substituted a simple deed, executed by the tenant in tail and enrolled in Chancery within six calendar months, for both a fine and a recovery. But it was thought desirable, in the case of tenant in tail in remainder, to alter the check which the ancient law imposed on his barring remainders (*o*), and to impose a new check of a similar kind, but of a nature more suitable to the requirements of the case. This was done by establishing the office of *protector* of the settlement, who now stands generally in the place of the ancient tenant for life. The technical rule requiring the concurrence of the person seised of the freehold in possession is abolished; and the consent of the protector is required to be obtained, in order to enable a tenant in tail in remainder to create a larger estate than a base fee, that is to say, to enable him to bar the remainders or reversion expectant on his estate tail. But as he might under the old law have barred his issue by a fine (*p*), so under the present law he may bar his own issue without the consent of the protector. The act, as we have seen (*q*), in the 15th section, empowers every actual tenant in tail in possession, remainder, contingency or otherwise, to convey an estate in fee simple. And this power is subject to the exceptions, which I mentioned in my last Lecture (*r*), with regard to women tenants in tail *ex provisione viri* under former settlements, and to estates tail belonging to tenants in tail created by the crown for the reward of public services, and also to tenants in tail after possibility of issue extinct. The act then provides (*s*) that after the 31st of December, 1833, in every case in which an estate tail in lands shall have been barred and converted into

Protector.

Power to enlarge a base fee.

(*n*) Ante, pp. 161—164.
(*o*) Ante, p. 170.
(*p*) Ante, p. 172.
(*q*) Ante, p. 161.
(*r*) Ante, p. 162.
(*s*) Sect. 19.

a *base fee*, either before or on or after that day, the person who, if such estate tail had not been barred, would have been actual tenant in tail of the same lands, shall have full power to dispose of such lands, as against all persons, including the crown, whose estates are to take effect after the determination or in defeasance of the base fee, into which the estate tail shall have been converted, *so as to enlarge the base fee into a fee simple absolute*, saving always the rights of all persons in respect of estates prior to the estate tail which shall have been converted into a base fee, and the rights of all other persons, except those against whom such disposition is by the act authorized to be made. But, as we shall see, the consent of the protector, if there is one, is required to be obtained, before any estate to take effect after the determination or in defeasance of an estate tail or base fee in remainder, can be barred.

Issue inheritable not to bar expectancies.

The act provides (*t*), that nothing in the act contained shall enable any person to dispose of any lands entailed in respect of any expectant interest, which he may have as issue inheritable to an estate tail therein. Before this act, a person, who was heir apparent or heir presumptive to an estate tail, might have bound his expectant interest by levying a fine. Now he cannot do so.

Protector.

The act further enacts (*u*), that if at the time when there shall be a tenant in tail of lands under a settlement, there shall be subsisting in the same lands or any of them, *under the same settlement*, any estate for years determinable on the dropping of a life or lives, or any greater estate (not being an estate for years), prior to the estate tail, then the person who shall be the owner of the prior estate, or the first of such prior estates if more than one, then subsisting *under the same settlement*,

(*t*) Sect. 20.

(*u*) Sect. 22.

or who would have been so, if no absolute disposition thereof had been made (the first of such prior estates, if more than one, being for all the purposes of the act deemed the prior estate), shall be the protector of the settlement so far as regards the lands in which such prior estate shall be subsisting, and shall for all the purposes of the act be deemed the owner of such prior estate, although the same may have been charged or incumbered either by the owner thereof or by the settlor or otherwise howsoever, and although the whole of the rents and profits be exhausted or required for the payment of the charges and incumbrances on such prior estate, and although such prior estate may have been absolutely disposed of by the owner thereof, or by or in consequence of the bankruptcy or insolvency of such owner, or by any other act or default of such owner; and that an estate by the curtesy (*x*) in respect of the estate tail, or of any prior estate created by the same settlement, shall be deemed a prior estate under the same settlement within the meaning of this clause; and that an estate by way of resulting use or trust to or for the settlor (*y*) shall be deemed an estate under the same settlement within the meaning of this clause.

Tenant for years determinable on lives formerly took no part in a recovery.

This enactment differs very materially from the law as it existed before the passing of the act. Before the act, a tenant for a term of years determinable on the dropping of a life or lives, could not make the tenant to the præcipe or writ for suffering a common recovery; for a term of years, whether absolute or determinable on the dropping of a life or lives, or on any other event, is not a freehold. It is in law merely a chattel real. The tenant of such a term is not *seised;* and as the writ was required to be brought against the person who

(*x*) See Principles of the Law of Real Property, p. 227, 12th ed.

(*y*) See ibid., p. 158.

was *seised*, a tenant for a term of years determinable on lives had no voice or part in the suffering of a common recovery. But now, as you see, such a tenant for years determinable on lives, if his estate is prior to the estate tail, is the protector of the settlement. Under the old law also, if the tenant for life had aliened his estate, and so conveyed the legal seisin to a third person, the concurrence of that third person was necessary before a recovery could be suffered. But now the owner of a prior estate for life, or for years determinable on lives, is the protector, notwithstanding he may have disposed of his estate absolutely, or charged or incumbered it to any extent.

Alienee of tenant for life.

Protector's estate must be under the same settlement.

There is also a material alteration in this respect; that the person who is protector must be tenant for life, or for years determinable on lives, or for some greater estate, other than an estate for years, *under the same settlement*. This was not the case under the old law. It mattered not how the tenant for life became entitled to his estate: if he had the legal seisin, his concurrence was necessary, except in the case I have just mentioned of leases of lands to tenants for lives at rents; which case was especially provided for by the act of 14 George II. (z). But, under the present act, a tenant for life under a former settlement is not the protector, although he may have the legal seisin of the lands. This point was decided by the Court of Exchequer, and on appeal by the Court of Exchequer Chamber, in the case of *Berrington* v. *Scott and others*, in which I was counsel, and which is reported only in the *Law Times* (a). The case was this:—One Rhys Davies devised the lands, one-third of which was in question in the case, to his daughter Anne Perrott for life, with remainder, in the

Berrington v. *Scott.*

(z) Stat. 14 Geo. 2, c. 20, s. 1; ante, p. 170.

(a) Law Times, N. S., Vol. 32, p. 125.

event which happened, to his brother Jenkin Davies Berrington and his heirs for ever. Afterwards Jenkin Davies Berrington, in the lifetime of Anne Perrott, made his will, dated 7th of May, 1834, by which he devised one-third of the premises unto his son Rhys Davies Berrington and his heirs lawfully begotten; and in default of issue of Rhys Davies Berrington, he gave the same third part to his son Jenkin Davies Berrington the younger in fee; thus giving to Rhys Davies Berrington an estate in tail, with remainder in fee to Jenkin Davies Berrington. He then died in Anne Perrott's lifetime. Rhys Davies Berrington then executed disentailing deeds of lease and release (*b*) of the 1st and 2nd of August, 1838, whereby he, without the concurrence of Anne Perrott, the tenant for life under the will of Rhys Davies, who was still living, conveyed his third part of the lands in question to a third person and his heirs, to the use of himself, his heirs and assigns for ever; and these deeds were duly enrolled in the Court of Chancery within six calendar months (*c*). Anne Perrott died on the 31st March, 1872; and the question was, whether the disentailing deeds, which were executed by Rhys Davies Berrington without the consent of Anne Perrott, were effectual to cut off the remainder in fee given by the will of Jenkin Davies Berrington to his son Jenkin Davies Berrington the younger. And it was unanimously decided, both by the Court of Exchequer and by the Court of Exchequer Chamber, that the consent of Anne Perrott was unnecessary; that the statute required the protector to be a person entitled to a prior estate *under the same settlement;* and that here the settlement was not the same. Anne Perrott was entitled to her life estate under the will of Rhys Davies; but Rhys Davies Berrington was entitled to his estate in tail under the will of Jenkin

(*b*) Ante, p. 146. (*c*) Ante. pp. 161—164.

Davies Berrington the elder. The settlements therefore were distinct; and as by the will of Jenkin Davies Berrington the elder the one-third was devised directly to Rhys Davies Berrington in tail, without the intervention of any prior estate, Rhys Davies Berrington had power, under the act, to alien his one-third devised to him for an estate in fee simple, which he did. The proceedings were in the form of a special case, which came on to be heard on the 18th of January, 1875, before Mr. Baron Cleasby, Mr. Baron Amphlett, and Mr. Baron Pollock, who gave judgment for the defendant, who claimed under the disentailing deed; and on appeal to the Exchequer Chamber on the 24th of June, 1875, their judgment was affirmed.

Protector where two or more owners.

Where there are two or more owners of an estate sufficient to confer the office of protector, the 23rd section provides that each of such persons, in respect of such undivided share as he could dispose of, shall be the sole protector of such settlement to the extent of such share. And the 24th section provides, that where a married woman would, if single, be the protector of a settlement in respect of a prior estate not settled or agreed to be settled to her separate use, she and her husband together shall, in respect of such estate, be the protector of the settlement, and shall be deemed one owner; but if such prior estate shall, by such settlement, have been settled, or agreed or directed to be settled, to her separate use, then she alone shall, in respect of such estate, be the protector of the settlement. This clause was held by V.-C. Wood, now Lord Hatherley, to apply to settlements executed before the passing of the act. The case of *Keer* v. *Brown* (*d*), in which this point was decided, contains an able exposition of the act.

Married woman.

(*d*) Johnson, 138.

The act provides (*e*), in analogy to the provisions made by the statute 14 George II. before referred to (*f*), that where a lease at a rent shall be created or confirmed by a settlement, the person in whose favour such lease shall be created or confirmed shall not, in respect thereof, be the protector of such settlement. But (*g*), except in the case of such a lease, where an estate shall be confirmed or restored by a settlement, such estate shall, for the purposes of the act, so far as regards the protector of the settlement, be deemed an estate subsisting under the settlement. The act further provides (*h*), that no woman in respect of her dower, no bare trustee, heir, executor, administrator, or assign, shall, in respect of any estate taken by him as such bare trustee, heir, executor, administrator or assign, be the protector of the settlement. From this provision is excepted (*i*) the case of a bare trustee, under a settlement made previously to the act. The reason of this exception is, that, previously to the act, it was not unfrequently the case that it was thought desirable to take away from the beneficial tenant for life the power of consenting to the suffering of a recovery, and to give it to trustees. In that case, nothing but a chattel interest for a term of years determinable on his own life was given to the person intended to be the beneficial owner during his life, and the freehold or legal seisin was vested in trustees during his life. They, therefore, were the persons to make the tenant to the præcipe, so that, without their concurrence, no recovery could be suffered. If, under the present act, a person wishes to appoint trustees to be protectors, he must do it by virtue of the provision contained in the 32nd section of the act, to which I shall presently refer.

Lessee at a rent.

Estate confirmed or restored.

Doweress, bare trustee, &c.

Bare trustee under previous settlement.

(*e*) Sect. 26.

(*f*) Stat. 14 Geo. 2, c. 20, s. 1; ante, p. 170.

(*g*) Sect. 25.

(*h*) Sect. 27.

(*i*) Sect. 31.

Where there are more than one estate prior to an estate tail.

The act further provides (*k*) to the effect that where, under any settlement, there shall be more than one estate prior to an estate tail, and the person who shall be the owner, within the meaning of the act, of any such prior estate, shall be excluded from being protector by being a lessee at a rent, or a doweress, bare trustee, heir, executor, administrator, or assign, then the person, if any, who, if such estate did not exist, would be protector of the settlement, shall be such protector. So that, in case of a lease at a rent, the lessee being excluded by the clause above mentioned, the protectorship of the settlement is determined just as if his estate did not exist. There are two clauses in the act (*l*) which provide for dispositions made previously thereto, and which are not now of any permanent interest.

Power for settlor to appoint protector.

The 32nd section of the act empowers the settlor to appoint a protector. And this act, unlike some other acts of parliament, is so accurately drawn that I cannot do better than give you the very words of the section. They are as follows:—"Provided always, and be it further enacted, that it shall be lawful for any settlor entailing lands to appoint by the settlement, by which the lands shall be entailed, any number of persons in esse, not exceeding three, and not being aliens, to be protector of the settlement in lieu of the person who would have been the protector if this clause had not been inserted, and either for the whole or any part of the period for which such person might have continued protector, and by means of a power to be inserted in such settlement to perpetuate during the whole or any part of such period the protectorship of the settlement in any one person or number of persons in esse, and not being an alien or aliens, whom the donee of the power shall think proper by deed to appoint protector of the settlement in the place of any one person or number of persons who shall die,

(*k*) Sect. 28.

(*l*) Sects. 29 and 30.

or shall by deed relinquish his or their office of protector; and the person or persons so appointed shall, in case of there being no other person then protector of the settlement, be the protector, and shall, in case of there being any other person then protector of the settlement, be protector jointly with such other person: Provided, nevertheless, that by virtue or means of any such appointment the number of the persons to compose the protector shall never exceed three: Provided further, nevertheless, that every deed by which a protector shall be appointed under a power in a settlement, and every deed by which a protector shall relinquish his office, shall be void unless enrolled in his Majesty's High Court of Chancery within six calendar months after the execution thereof: Provided further, nevertheless, that the person who but for this clause would have been sole protector of the settlement may be one of the persons to be appointed protector under this clause, if the settlor shall think fit; and shall, unless otherwise directed by the settlor, act as sole protector if the other persons constituting the protector shall have ceased to be so by death or relinquishment of the office by deed, and no other person shall have been appointed in their place." The act contains (*m*) provisions, which I need hardly state in detail, for the lunacy, idiotcy, or the unsoundness of mind of a protector; or for his being convicted of treason or felony, or being an infant, or for its being uncertain whether he is living or dead, or for no protector being appointed or in existence during the continuance of a prior estate.

The act provides (*n*), that if, at the time when any person, actual tenant in tail of lands under a settlement, but not entitled to the remainder or reversion in fee immediately expectant on the determination of his estate tail, shall be desirous of making, under the act, **Consent of protector required to bar remainders.**

(*m*) Sect. 33.

(*n*) Sect. 34.

a disposition of the lands entailed, there shall be a protector of such settlement, then the *consent of the protector shall be requisite* to enable such tenant in tail to dispose of the lands entailed, to the full extent to which he is before authorized to dispose of the same:—that is, in fact, to dispose of the same in fee simple. But such tenant in tail may, without such consent, make a disposition which shall be good against all persons claiming under the estate tail, that is, in other words, against the issue in tail. This provision corresponds generally to the ancient law, under which a tenant in tail in remainder might, with the concurrence of the tenant for life, suffer a recovery, and acquire the fee (*o*); but, without such concurrence, could only levy a fine, and acquire a base fee, to endure so long as there were any issue in tail remaining (*p*). The act also provides (*q*), that where an estate tail shall have been converted in a *base fee*, in such case, so long as there shall be a protector of the settlement, by which the estate tail was created, the *consent of such protector shall be requisite* to enable the person, who would have been tenant of the estate tail, if the same had not been barred, to exercise, as to the lands in respect of which there shall be such protector, the power of disposition thereinbefore contained. The two next sections (*r*), provide, that the protector shall be subject to no control in the exercise of his power of consenting, and shall not be amenable to a Court of Equity in respect of any dealing or transaction between himself and the tenant in tail, upon the occasion of his giving consent to a disposition under the act. So that the protector may make any bargain he pleases as to giving his consent, or he may give or withhold it entirely as he thinks fit.

Consent of protector required to enlargement of a base fee.

Protector under no control.

I mentioned (*s*), that under the ancient law, if a base

(*o*) Ante, p. 170.
(*p*) Ante, p. 172.
(*q*) Sect. 35.
(*r*) Sects. 36 and 37.
(*s*) Ante, p. 172.

fee in lands, and the remainder or reversion in fee in the same lands, became vested in the same person, the base fee merged in the remainder or reversion in fee. This rule is altered by the act (*t*), which provides that, in this case, if there is no intermediate estate, the base fee shall not merge, but shall be *ipso facto* enlarged into as large an estate as the tenant in tail, with the consent of the protector, if any, might have created by any disposition under the act, if such remainder or reversion had been vested in any other person. The effect of this enactment is, that the reversion in fee, instead of coming into immediate possession by the merger of the base fee, is thrust out and destroyed by the enlargement of the base fee into an estate in fee simple; so that incumbrances on the reversion, instead of being let into possession, are entirely destroyed; and incumbrances on the base fee, instead of being destroyed, are made incumbrances on the fee simple.

Base fee enlarged by union with remainder in fee.

The consent of the protector is to be given (*u*) either by the same assurance, by which the disposition shall be effected, or by a deed distinct from the assurance, and to be executed either on or at any time before the day on which the assurance shall be made, otherwise the consent shall be void. But (*x*) if the consent is by a distinct deed, it is considered to be absolute and unqualified, unless the protector in such deed refer to the particular assurance, by which the disposition shall be effected, and shall confine his consent to the disposition thereby made. And no protector who has once given his consent to a disposition by a tenant in tail, can afterwards revoke such consent (*y*). A married woman, being protector of a settlement, either alone or jointly with her husband, may consent to the disposition of the tenant in tail in the same manner as if she were a

Consent how given.

Consent irrevocable.

Married woman.

(*t*) Sect. 39.
(*u*) Sect. 42.
(*x*) Sect. 43.
(*y*) Sect. 44.

Consent by deed to be enrolled.

feme sole (z). So that whenever she concurs with her husband in any deed merely for the purpose of consenting as protector to a disposition by a tenant in tail, there is no occasion for the deed to be separately acknowledged by her, under the provisions for that purpose contained in the same act. But it is provided (*a*) that the consent of a protector to the disposition of a tenant in tail shall, if given by deed distinct from the assurance by which the disposition shall be effected by the tenant in tail, be void unless such deed be enrolled in the High Court of Chancery (now represented by the Chancery Division of the High Court), either at or before the time when the assurance shall be enrolled. You may remember (*b*) that every assurance by a tenant in tail (except such a lease for years as is mentioned in the act) must be enrolled in the Chancery Division of the High Court within six calendar months after the execution thereof. The act (*c*) entirely excludes the jurisdiction of Courts of Equity, and also provides that no disposition by a tenant in tail in equity, and no consent by a protector to a disposition of lands by a tenant in tail in equity, shall be of any force, unless such disposition or consent would, in case of an estate tail at law, be an effectual disposition or consent under the act in a court of law. So that in all cases, whether the estates are legal or equitable, the formalities required by the act must be observed; and if they are not observed, no intention to do so will be sufficient, nor will any mistake or inadvertence be remedied in equity.

Equity excluded.

Equitable tenant in tail.

Confirmation of voidable estate of a purchaser.

The 38th section of the act contains a valuable provision, the effect of which is, that a voidable estate created by a tenant in tail in favour of a *purchaser* for valuable consideration is confirmed by any subsequent disposition made by such tenant in tail under the act;

(*z*) Sect. 45.

(*a*) Sect. 46.

(*b*) Sect. 41; ante, p. 164.

(*c*) Sect. 47.

except as against a subsequent purchaser for valuable consideration, who shall not have express notice of the voidable estate. The case of *Crocker* v. *Waine* (*d*) contains a valuable exposition of this section of the statute.

Copyholds.

With regard to copyholds, the consent of the protector may be given either to the person taking the surrender made by the tenant in tail, or by deed to be executed and produced to the lord of the manor, or the steward or his deputy, at or before the time when the surrender is made, and to be entered on the court rolls. I mentioned (*e*) that a tenant in tail of copyholds, whose estate is an estate in equity only, may bar his estate tail either by surrender, or by deed to be entered on the court rolls within six calendar months. If there is in this case a protector, his consent may be given, either by the same deed, or by a distinct deed, to be executed by the protector either on or at any time before the day on which the deed of disposition shall be executed by the equitable tenant in tail, and to be entered on the court rolls. And the act provides that every such deed of disposition by an equitable tenant in tail shall be void against any person claiming the lands for valuable consideration under any subsequent assurance duly entered on the court rolls, unless the deed of disposition be entered on the court rolls before the subsequent assurance shall have been entered. The sections relating to copyholds are sects. 50 to 54 inclusive.

Quasi estates tail.

I mentioned in my last Lecture (*f*) that quasi estates tail may exist in estates *pur autre vie*, and also in equity in the right or expectation of renewal in all cases where such right or expectation exists. I also mentioned (*g*) that the same estates may exist in copyholds, where the custom of the manor admits at law of no

(*d*) 5 Best & Smith, 697.

(*e*) Ante, p. 165.

(*f*) Ante, p. 166.

(*g*) Ante, p. 167.

greater estate than an estate for a life or lives, with or without the right or expectation of renewal. I also mentioned that these quasi estates if in possession might be barred, in the case of freeholds, by a deed of conveyance *inter vivos*, and in the case of copyholds by a surrender *inter vivos;* but in neither case by will. I also stated that the Act for the Abolition of Fines and Recoveries had no application to these estates. But a quasi estate tail may be in remainder expectant on an estate for life. Thus, renewable leaseholds for lives may be settled on A. for life, with remainder to B. and the heirs of his body, with remainders over. So, copyholds for lives may be settled in the same manner. In these cases the analogy of the law, as it stood when recoveries and fines were suffered and levied, is still followed. B., the tenant in tail in remainder, may bar his own issue by alienation *inter vivos* by deed or surrender, as the case may be. But he cannot bar the remainders over otherwise than by deed or surrender *inter vivos*, made with the concurrence of the owner of A.'s life estate (*h*).

Quasi estates tail in remainder.

I have thus endeavoured to show how the seisin of the freehold, under the old law, played an important part in regulating the barring of estates tail, and how, in modern times, improved means have been devised for this purpose. In my next Lecture I hope to point out the effect which the seisin of the freehold has had, and in some cases still has, on *contingent remainders*, including in them estates given to *unborn* persons, which estates are now the ordinary means used for the settlement of lands.

(*h*) *Allen* v. *Allen*, 2 Dru. & War. 307; *Edwards* v. *Champion*, 3 De Gex, M. & G. 202.

LECTURE XII.

WE now come to consider the seisin of the freehold as it affects contingent remainders.

Special tail, ancient mode of settlement.

I mentioned in a former Lecture (a) that down to the time of the Commonwealth, the usual mode of making family settlements was by means of a gift in *special tail*, to the husband and wife and to the heirs of their bodies begotten. Sometimes the limitation was varied by making it to the husband and wife and to the heirs of the body of the husband; and sometimes to the husband and wife and to the heirs of the body of the wife. But the estates given appear to have been uniformly *vested estates tail* given to living persons, and not estates tail given in remainder to sons or daughters not yet born.

In a paper which I read before the Juridical Society on the 21st of May, 1855 (b), I stated that I had made several searches, for the purpose of ascertaining when the now universal method of settlement of real estates first came into use. This method gives an estate for life, in the case of a marriage settlement, to the husband, and sometimes also to the wife, with remainder to the first and every other son, to be born of the marriage, severally and successively, one after the other, and to the heirs male of their respective bodies, the elder of such sons, and the heirs male of his body, always to be preferred and to take before the younger of such sons and the heirs male of his body. The result of my searches is that I have not been able to discover

(a) Ante, pp. 152, 153. (b) Juridical Papers, 1855, p. 45.

Unborn sons.

any trace of a limitation of an estate tail, or any other estate, to an unborn son, prior to the third and fourth years of the reign of Philip and Mary. I discovered two settlements made in those years giving estates for the life of the parents, with remainder to the use of the first begotten son or first male issue (which is the same thing) of the husband, and the heirs of the body of the said first begotten son or first male issue, with remainders over to the several younger sons or issues male of the husband, and the heirs of their several bodies lawfully begotten. One of these settlements was the subject of dispute in *Chudleigh's case*, called also the case of perpetuities (*c*). In each of these cases the settlement was made by way of use under the Statute of Uses. In Chudleigh's case a feoffment was made to several feoffees, their heirs and assigns for ever, to the use of the feoffees, their heirs and assigns during the life of Christopher Chudleigh, the eldest son of the feoffor, with remainder to the use of the first issue male of the said Christopher Chudleigh lawfully to be begotten, and the heirs of the body of such first issue male lawfully to be begotten, and so on to the second, third and other issues male of the said Christopher Chudleigh and the heirs of their respective bodies lawfully to be begotten. I believe that these settlements were made on the supposition that, as the contingent estates were created by virtue of the Statute of Uses (*d*), which, as you remember, was passed for the turning of uses into possession, that statute would have the effect of preserving the contingent remainders to the unborn issue from being destroyed by any act of the tenant for life, or otherwise. In this, however, the settlors were disappointed, as we shall presently see.

Chudleigh's case.

In order to understand this subject, it is first neces-

(*c*) 1 Co. Rep. 113 *b*.

(*d*) Stat. 27 Hen. 8, c. 10; ante, p. 137.

sary to get a clear idea of what a contingent remainder is. The contingency of a remainder does not depend, as might at first sight be thought, upon the uncertainty of its ever coming into possession. Thus, if lands be given to A., a young man of twenty-one, for his life, and after his decease to his father B., a man of seventy, for his life, it is obvious that there is a great contingency as to whether B., the father, will ever come into possession of the estates; nevertheless, B. the father, has a vested estate for life in remainder. And the reason is, that if the estate of his son should cease by his death, or by any other means, as by forfeiture of his estate, or by his surrendering it to B. during the life of B., B.'s estate is always *capable of coming into immediate possession* on the termination of the estate of A. It is the *capacity for coming into immediate possession* if the prior estate should at any moment determine which distinguishes a vested from a contingent remainder. According to this rule, you will see that an estate, of which great use was made in conveyancing until comparatively recent times, is a vested and not a contingent estate. That is this:—A conveyance to A. for his life, and, after the determination of his estate by forfeiture or otherwise in his lifetime, to B. and his heirs during the life of A. This estate given to B. is considered in law to be a vested estate; because, if the estate of A. should at any time determine, the estate of B. has always a capacity for coming into immediate possession (*e*). But an estate given to an unborn person is evidently contingent. Thus, if lands be given to A., a bachelor, for his life, on his marriage, with remainder to his eldest son and the heirs of the body of such eldest son, this remainder is contingent until A. has a son; but after he has had a son, the remainder becomes a vested remainder in that son and the heirs

A contingent remainder.

A vested remainder.

Example.

Estate given to an unborn son.

(*e*) See Principles of the Law of Real Property, pp. 267, 268, 283 (12th ed.).

male of his body. After the birth of the son the lands are limited to A. for his life, with a vested remainder in his eldest son in tail. Under the old law the eldest son might, on his coming of age, with the concurrence of A. his father, the tenant of the freehold, have suffered a common recovery, and acquired the fee simple (*f*). Or he might, without the concurrence of A., have levied a fine, and so barred his own issue, and acquired an estate to him and his heirs so long as that issue lasted (*g*). But, before the birth of the son, the contingent estate given to him, in case he should be born, was in very great peril. It was liable to destruction in several ways; and, in fact, in ancient times it seems to have been at least doubtful whether it was lawful to create any contingent remainder. I have given my reasons for supposing that, by the better opinion, such remainders could not anciently have been created, in the chapter on Contingent Remainders in my Principles of the Law of Real Property (*h*). However, in process of time, such contingent remainders were recognized (*i*); but it was of very little use to create them, because they were destructible in several ways. Thus, if the tenant for life, on whose decease a remainder was contingent, made a feoffment, levied a fine, or suffered a common recovery, in each case the contingent remainder was entirely destroyed, and could not be again revived, even though the event afterwards happened on which the contingent remainder was to take effect. Thus, in the case I have given of lands being settled on A. for life, with remainder to his eldest unborn son in tail, A. was able, before he had a son, by feoffment, fine or recovery, altogether to destroy the contingent remainder to his eldest son; so that the eldest son when born found himself without any provision whatever.

Whether contingent remainders anciently lawful.

Destruction of contingent remainder by feoffment, fine, or recovery.

(*f*) Ante, p. 170.

(*g*) Ante, p. 172.

(*h*) Pages 263, 264 (12th ed.).

(*i*) *Colthirst* v. *Bejushin*, Plow. 21.

Forfeiture.

The feoffment, fine or recovery in this case operated as a forfeiture of the life estate of A., in favour of the person entitled to the *next vested estate*, as distinguished from the next contingent estate in remainder. But it might be, and it often was, that A., the tenant for life, was himself entitled to the immediate reversion in fee expectant on the determination of the estates tail given in contingency to his first and other sons successively. In this case a feoffment, fine or common recovery, made, levied or suffered by him to his own use simply gave him the fee simple absolute, free from all the contingent remainders. In the case, then, of a gift to A. for life, with remainder to his first and other sons successively in tail, with remainder to himself in fee, the law allowed the contingent remainders to have their chance of taking effect, until, by any subsequent event, they should be destroyed; and such subsequent event might be, as I have said, a feoffment, fine or recovery made, levied or suffered by A. Or the destruction of the contingent remainders might have happened by A. conveying his life estate and his ultimate remainder in fee to a third person, B. In such a case, B. would acquire the life estate of A., and also the remainder in fee expectant on his life estate, which two estates make up the whole fee simple. The life estate, in such a case, would be said to be *merged* or drowned in the remainder in fee. And by this means the contingent remainder was destroyed. Conveyances of this kind, made for the express purpose of destroying contingent remainders to unborn children, were by no means of unusual occurrence.

Merger of life estate.

Surrender of life estate.

Again, suppose lands to have been settled on A. for life, with remainder to his first and other unborn sons successively in tail, with remainder to B. in fee. There was nothing to prevent A., the moment that such a settlement was made, from giving up or *surrendering* his life estate to B. (*k*). In this case, B.'s remainder in fee simple would come into immediate possession; and, by this means also, the contingent remainders to the sons of A. would be destroyed.

It was evidently, therefore, in this state of circumstances, almost useless for any person to attempt to create a contingent remainder. And it was not till after the passing of the Statute of Uses that a device was hit upon for the preservation of contingent remainders to unborn children. The first device appears to have been, the creation of the contingent remainders to the unborn children by the means of the Statute of Uses (*l*), which statute had the effect of turning all uses into estates in possession. This was the plan tried in *Chudleigh's case*, to which I have just referred. It appears to have been thought that, as the statute gave to those that had the use the same estate that they had in the use, the use limited to the first male issue could not be destroyed by a feoffment made by the feoffees who were the tenants of the freehold during the life of Christopher Chudleigh. In this case, however, the feoffees, prior to the birth of any son of Christopher Chudleigh, made a feoffment of the lands to him in fee simple; after which he had two sons born. And it was decided that, although the limitations to his eldest and second son were by way of use, yet that the feoffment so made by the feoffees to uses, who had the legal seisin during the life of Christopher Chudleigh, destroyed the contingent remainders to his issue male. The court seems to have thought that to decide otherwise would tend to cause lands to remain in settlement for too long a time. Hence the case was called *the case of perpetuities*. And some of the arguments of the

Chudleigh's case.

Feoffment by owners of first life estate.

(*k*) Ante, p. 121.

(*l*) Stat. 27 Hen. 8, c. 10; ante, p. 137.

judges (*m*) are much the same as those which, in the present day, are directed against the modern method of settling lands, against which method they set their faces, and for a time with success. A contingent remainder, created by way of use, was deliberately left, by this decision, in the same helpless condition, as if it had been created at the common law, without the intervention of the Statute of Uses.

The first person who hit upon an effectual means for the preservation of contingent remainders appears to have been Sir Orlando Bridgman, who, being a staunch Royalist, betook himself to chamber practice as a conveyancer in the time of the Commonwealth. On the restoration of King Charles II. he became successively Lord Chief Baron of the Exchequer, Lord Chief Justice of the Court of Common Pleas, and Lord Keeper of the Great Seal. His precedents were collected by Mr. Johnson, his clerk, and are now preserved in three folio volumes, usually bound in one. In the first volume (*n*) will be found a precedent of a marriage settlement. It is made by lease and release. It begins by reciting the intended solemnization of the marriage; and then recites, that the intended husband, the better to enable him to grant release and convey the hereditaments, had, by an indenture of bargain and sale dated the day before, in consideration of 5*s.*, bargained and sold the lands to the father and brother of the intended wife for one year. It then witnesses that, in consideration of the marriage, the intended husband releases the premises unto the father and brother of the intended wife, their heirs and assigns, to the use of the intended husband during his natural life without impeachment of waste, and from and after the determination of that estate to the use of two brothers of the intended wife their heirs and assigns for and during all the time of the natural

Sir Orlando Bridgman.

A marriage settlement.

(*m*) 1 Rep. 138 b, 139 a.

(*n*) Page 83.

Trust to preserve contingent remainders.

life of the said intended husband, upon trust only for the preserving the contingent uses and estates thereinafter limited, and to make entries for the same, if the same should be needful. But that the said two brothers their heirs and assigns should not convert the rents, issues or profits thereof to their own use. And from and immediately after the death of the said intended husband, a jointure is given to the wife. And, subject thereto, the settlement proceeds, after the decease of the said intended husband, "to the use and behoof of the first son of the said (intended husband) and the heirs male of the body of such first son lawfully to be begotten, and in default of such issue to the use and behoof of the second son of the said (intended husband) and the heirs male of his body," and so forth, with remainder to the use and behoof of the right heirs of the said intended husband for ever.

Now this device would not have been effectual, had it not been for a decision of the courts of law, with respect to the Statute of Uses, by which the intent of that statute was practically set aside. When a use was turned into a legal estate by the Statute of Uses, it was said to be *executed* (o); so that a conveyance of lands to A. and his heirs to the use of or in trust for B. and his heirs, left nothing whatever in A., but vested the whole fee simple in B. But it was held that the statute had no operation on a second use or trust limited after the first use or trust. A use, it was quaintly said, could not be engendered of a use. So that if lands were conveyed to A. and his heirs, to the use of B. and his heirs, to the use of C. and his heirs, or if lands were conveyed to A. and his heirs, upon trust for B. and his heirs, upon trust for C. and his heirs, in both these cases it was decided, that the statute executed, or turned into a legal estate,

First use only executed.

(o) Ante, p. 141.

only the first use or trust to B. and his heirs, and left the third or ultimate use or trust for C. and his heirs quite unaffected by the statute.

Trusts.

Trusts, therefore, were, by this doctrine, again re-established, contrary to the obvious intent of the act, which clearly was to put an end to them all. In the settlement, therefore, which I have mentioned, the effect of the limitations was this. By the bargain and sale, or lease for a year, the father and brother of the intended wife were put, by the Statute of Uses, into immediate actual possession of the premises, and were thus rendered capable of receiving a release by deed of the fee simple (*p*). By the release which followed they obtained the seisin of the freehold, which was however but momentary; for the Statute of Uses again interfered and transferred into possession the use to which they were declared to be seised. By virtue of the limitation *to the use* of the husband for life, without impeachment of waste, he had, under the Statute of Uses, an estate at law in the lands, in immediate possession or seisin, for his life without impeachment of waste. By virtue of the limitation to the use and behoof of the two brothers of the wife, their heirs and assigns during the natural life of the husband, upon trust for preserving the contingent uses or estates, but not to convert the rents or profits to their own use, these two brothers had immediately a vested estate of freehold in remainder during the life of the husband, expectant on the termination of the life estate of the husband by any means during his life (*q*). Their trust was, to make entries for preserving the contingent estates, if the same should be needful. Now this trust, by virtue of the doctrine to which I have just adverted, was a trust enforceable in equity. They had a vested estate for life in remainder given to them; but not for their own use,

Trust to preserve contingent remainders.

(*p*) Ante, pp. 119, 120, 146.

(*q*) Ante, p. 189.

by reason of the subsequent or second use or trust engrafted on the estate given to them, which prevented them from converting the profits to their own use. If, therefore, under these circumstances, the husband had made a feoffment, levied a fine, or suffered a common recovery of the lands, such feoffment, fine or recovery would have been a cause of forfeiture, as we have seen (*r*), to the persons entitled to the next vested estate. Now, in our case, the persons entitled to the next vested estate, were the two brothers of the wife; and it would have been their duty, in such a case, immediately to enter upon the lands, by reason of the forfeiture, and to hold the same, during the rest of the life of the husband, for the purpose of preserving the contingent uses or estates limited by the settlement. An actual entry on their parts would not, however, have been absolutely necessary; for it was held that a *right of entry* subsisting in respect of a prior estate of freehold was sufficient to preserve a contingent remainder. So, if the husband conveyed his life estate, and also the ultimate remainder in fee given to him by the settlement, to a third person and his heirs, such conveyance would not have destroyed the contingent remainders to his first and other sons successively in tail male, for the two brothers of the wife had a vested estate subsisting in them, and standing between the life estate of the husband on the one part and the reversion in fee belonging to him on the other part. If, therefore, these two estates were conveyed to a third person, the life estate would not merge in the reversion in fee, because there was a vested estate between the two, which kept them apart. The contingent remainders, therefore, would not have been destroyed by such a conveyance. For the same reason, if the ultimate reversion had belonged to any one else, no surrender of the husband's life estate could have been made by him

Feoffment, fine, or recovery by husband.

Entry.

Right of entry.

Conveyance of life estate and remainder in fee to same person.

No surrender of life estate when a vested estate intervenes.

(*r*) Ante, p. 191.

to the person entitled to the reversion or remainder in fee, for a surrender is the giving up of a particular estate to the person entitled to the *next immediate* vested interest in remainder or reversion; and the persons in this case who were entitled to the next immediate estate in remainder were the two brothers of the wife. By this device, therefore, the contingent remainders were effectually preserved, so long as the trustees to preserve them were faithful to their trust. It is true that, had they proved faithless to their trust, they might have concurred with the tenant for life in destroying the contingent remainders by feoffment, fine, or recovery; but, had they done so, they would have been personally answerable, in equity, to the eldest son, when born, for the breach of trust they had committed (*s*). By this means, therefore, contingent remainders to unborn children were preserved, whilst they were contingent, until they became vested estates; after which, they could not be destroyed by any of the methods above spoken of. They might have been turned into rights of action; but still by an action they might have been recovered.

Thus the law continued until the passing of the Act to amend the Law of Real Property (*t*). By this act the necessity for trustees to preserve contingent remainders was done away with. For it enacts (*u*), that a contingent remainder, existing at any time after the 31st day of December, 1844, shall be, and, if created before the passing of the act, shall be deemed to have been, capable of taking effect, notwithstanding the determination by forfeiture, surrender or merger of any preceding estate of freehold, in the same manner in all respects as if such determination had not happened. The act also provides, as we have seen (*x*), that a feoff-

Contingent remainders protected from forfeiture, surrender or merger of particular estate.

(*s*) *Biscoe* v. *Perkins*, 1 Ves. & B. 485, 491.

(*t*) Stat. 8 & 9 Vict. c. 106.

(*u*) Sect. 8.

(*x*) Sect. 4; ante, pp. 102, 105, 106.

ment, made after the 1st day of October, 1845, shall not have any tortious operation. By this enactment, therefore, irrespective of the 8th section, no feoffment could, after that time, have destroyed a contingent remainder; and, as you may remember, fines and recoveries had been abolished by the act of 3 & 4 Will. IV. c. 74 (*y*). So that forfeiture of a life estate by these means had become impossible. Nevertheless, contingent remainders might have been destroyed by surrender or merger of the prior life estate, in the absence of an intervening estate to trustees for the purpose of preserving them. But by this enactment a contingent remainder is set up or preserved, and allowed its chance of taking effect, so long as the prior estate of freehold would have continued, if it had not been determined by the means above-mentioned.

Vesting of a contingent remainder.

The law, however, respecting the seisin of the freehold, required that a contingent remainder of an estate of freehold should become a vested estate, either at or before the expiration of the prior estate of freehold. The contingent remainder could not be made to take effect as a vested remainder, after the expiration of the prior estate of freehold. The law required that the seisin should be notorious and continuous; so that, if lands were given to A. for life, with remainder on a contingency, it should be known on or before the death of A. who was the next person to become seised in possession. If the next vested estate once came into possession, the contingent estate was for ever lost and defeated. A doubt therefore arose as to what would happen in the case of an estate given to A. for life, with remainder to his eldest son, if A. were to die and leave his wife *enceinte* of a son. Would the contingent remainder to the son fail to take effect, by reason of his

Tenant for life dying, leaving his wife *enceinte*.

(*y*) Ante, p. 161.

not being in existence to enter upon the estate immediately on the decease of his father? This doubt was remedied by a statute of 10 & 11 of Will. III. (z). This act is intituled "An Act to enable posthumous Children to take Estates as if born in their Father's lifetime." It recites that it often happens that by marriage and other settlements estates are limited in remainder to the use of the sons and daughters, the issue of such marriage, with remainders over, without limiting an estate to trustees to preserve the contingent remainders limited to such sons and daughters, by which means such sons and daughters, if they happen to be born after the decease of their father, are in danger to be defeated of their remainder by the next in remainder after them, and left unprovided for by such settlements, contrary to the intent of the parties that made those settlements. And it enacts, in effect, that where any estate is limited in remainder to the use of the first or other son or sons of any person, with remainders over to any other persons, or to the use of a daughter or daughters, with any remainders over to any other persons, that any son or daughter lawfully begotten, who shall be born after the decease of his, her or their father, shall and may take such estate so limited, in the same manner as if born in the lifetime of the father, although there shall happen no estate to be limited to trustees, after the decease of the father, to preserve the contingent remainder to such after-born son or daughter, until he or she come *in esse* or is born to take the same.

Posthumous children enabled to take as if born.

This act, however, is confined to the particular case of posthumous children; and a contingent remainder is still liable to destruction, by the event of its not coming into possession on or before the determina-

Contingent remainders still liable to destruction.

(z) 10 & 11 Will. 3, c. 16.

tion of the particular estate of freehold, upon which it depends (*a*). The rule that a continuous seisin of the freehold must be provided for, is still in full operation, and occasionally produces the disastrous result of entirely defeating the intention of those who attempt to make settlements without a knowledge of the extremely technical rules on which such settlements depend (*a*).

Festing v. *Allen*.

A notable example of this occurred in the case of *Festing* v. *Allen* (*b*). In this case one Roger Belk, by his will, devised all his lands and real estates whatsoever to three persons, their heirs and assigns, *to the use* of his wife and her assigns for her life, if she should so long continue his widow and unmarried; and after her decease or marriage, to the use of his granddaughter Martha Hannah Johnson and her assigns for her life; and after her decease, to the use of all and every the child or children of her the said Martha Hannah Johnson *who should attain the age of twenty-one years*, if more than one, equally to be divided amongst them, share and share alike, as tenants in common, and to their respective heirs and assigns for ever. Under the limitation to the trustees and their heirs to the use of the widow during her life or widowhood, she took, by virtue of the Statute of Uses, an immediate legal estate on the death of her husband, during her life or widowhood, and the trustees had the whole fee simple immediately taken from them, just as if the gifts had been to the widow directly. So there was a legal vested remainder to Martha Hannah Johnson for her life, and a legal contingent remainder in fee to become a vested estate on any child attaining twenty-one and not before. The testator died in 1824. His widow died in the lifetime of M. H. Johnson. M. H. Johnson married Mr. Festing

(*a*) The law on this subject is happily now amended by Stat. 40 & 41 Vict. c. 33, which was passed after these Lectures were delivered, and a copy of which, with some remarks thereon, will be found in Appendix (B).

(*b*) 12 Mee. & Wels. 279.

in 1825, and died in the year 1833, leaving three children, John Belk Festing, Henry Festing and Thomas Festing, her only children, who were then infants of the respective ages of six years, three years, and one year, or thereabouts. And it was held that these three children, for whom the lands were undoubtedly intended, took nothing whatever by the devise to them. It was held to be clear that the limitations were defeated by the death of Mrs. Festing leaving no child who had then attained the age of twenty-one years. It was held, that the limitations to take effect at her decease were all of them contingent remainders in fee; and, if she had, at her decease, left a child who had *then* attained the age of twenty-one years, her child or children would have taken absolutely. But as there was, at her decease, no child who had attained twenty-one, the contingent remainders failed, and the whole property belonged to the heir-at-law of the testator.

Now, if the testator, instead of creating legal estates by means of single uses, had created a use upon a use, and had vested the whole property in the trustees, by simply giving it to them and their heirs, to the use of them and their heirs, upon trusts of a similar nature, equity would have preserved the contingent remainders to the children; and, on their coming of age, they would have been entitled to the land.

I cannot imagine a case more loudly crying for a reform in the law. The ancient rule that the seisin of the freehold must be notorious and continuous has long ceased to produce any beneficial effect; but, in cases of this sort, it has still been allowed to remain, doing no good whatever, but a great deal of mischief (*c*).

(*c*) But see now n. (*a*), ante, p. 200.

Copyholds.

With regard to copyholds, the law as to contingent remainders is not the same as with regard to freehold lands. The seisin, as you remember, is in the lord. The seisin vested in the lord is therefore said to preserve all contingent remainders limited in copyhold lands. A tenant for life of copyholds was therefore unable, by any act of his own, to destroy any contingent remainder in favour of his unborn issue or any other person. The analogy, however, to contingent remainders of freeholds, is carried out still to this extent:—that, if the contingent remainder does not become vested at or before the expiration of the particular estate of freehold, or rather of quasi freehold, it cannot become vested at all. In such a case therefore as that of *Festing* v. *Allen*, a surrender of copyhold lands to A. for life, with remainder to his children *who shall attain twenty-one*, creates a contingent remainder to such of the children as may attain twenty-one, which does not become vested until some child attains the age of twenty-one years. If they attain twenty-one in the lifetime of their parent, they will succeed him on his decease. But if, on his decease, they are under twenty-one, the contingent remainder fails to take effect, and the children, on attaining twenty-one, will find that they have become the victims of a technical rule (*d*).

I said in my first Lecture (*e*) that "some of our most remarkable laws of real property, viewed by themselves apart from their history, and judged only by the benefits that now result from them, appear to me to be absolutely worthless; others are worse than worthless, they are absurd and injurious." I think that I have now made good that proposition.

(*d*) But see now n. (*a*), ante, p. 200. (*e*) Page 1.

APPENDIX (A).

(Referred to pp. 136, 138.)

It will be observed that the statute 19 Hen. VII. c. 15, speaks of *heriots* due from the tenants of lands holden in socage to the lord, and that the Statute of Uses, 27 Hen. VIII. c. 10, speaks of *harriotts* being lost by the lords of manors by reason of feoffments to uses. A heriot or harriott, as it is generally spelt in old books, is generally the best beast, but sometimes the second best beast, sometimes the best chattel, and sometimes a sum of money belonging to a tenant, and becoming due to the lord, usually on the death of the tenant, but sometimes either on the death of the tenant or on his alienation.

Heriots service.

Heriots are divided into *heriots service* and *heriots custom*. Heriots service occur where heriots were reserved on the original grant of lands in fee, prior to the statute of *Quia emptores* (*a*). It is curious that heriots service are not mentioned by Littleton. Lord Coke, however, refers to them in his Commentaries on Littleton (*b*). And in his "Complete Copyholder" he says, that the Normans, "upon the parcelling of their lands unto inferior tenants, invented this new kind of service, unknown amongst the Saxons, and termed it by the name of *herriot service.* Afterwards, upon the enfranchisement and manumission of certain villeins, these heriot *customs* were given to the lords as a continual future gratulation" (*c*). Blackstone says (*d*), "An heriot may also appertain to free land, that is held by service and suit of court; in which case it is most commonly a copyhold enfranchised, whereupon the heriot is still due *by custom.*"

(*a*) Stat. 18 Edw. 1, c. 1, ante, p. 21.

(*b*) Co. Litt. 149 b, 185 b.

(*c*) Co. Cop., sec. 24; tracts, p. 25.

(*d*) 2 Bl. Comm., p. 424.

I have not been able to find any authority for this proposition. It does not seem to be borne out by the above passage from Coke's Copyholder. Heriot service and heriot custom are distinct. The one is in the nature of a rent reserved on the original grant of the lands in fee. The other is due by custom only, from every one of the lord's tenants, whether in fee or for any less estate. I think that Lord Coke intended to draw this distinction, saying that the Normans granted parts of their lands in fee to be held by *heriot service;* but that *heriot custom* arose when villeins holding their tenements by copy of court roll were manumitted and made free men.

Heriot custom.

Heriot service is said to lie both in *render* and in *prendre.* It lies in *render,* for it is in fact rent which may be distrained for. And it lies in *prendre,* because the lord may seize the heriot and take it away. Heriot custom lies in prendre only. It was at one time doubted whether heriot service did not lie exclusively in render; but it was long since decided that the lord may seize for heriot service as well as for heriot custom (*e*).

Heriots may be recovered by the lord of a manor, although he may by neglect have lost his quit rents by virtue of the Statute of Limitations, for the tenure remains (*f*). And it has been held that the lord's right to seize for heriot custom is not barred by his having neglected to seize on a former death, which occurred upwards of twenty years ago (*g*). The law with respect to heriots will be found at large in Scriven on Copyholds (*h*).

(*e*) *Woodland* v. *Mantel*, Plow. 94, 96.

(*f*) *Earl of Chichester* v. *Hall*, 17 Law Times, 121.

(*g*) *Lord Zouche* v. *Dalbiac*, L. R., 10 Ex. 172.

(*h*) Vol. 1, p. 437, 3rd ed.; p. 251, 5th ed.

APPENDIX (B).

(Referred to pp. 150, 200.)

THE following is the text of the Act to amend the Law as to Contingent Remainders (stat. 40 & 41 Vict. c. 33), passed 2nd August, 1877:—

"Be it enacted by the Queen's most excellent Majesty, by and with the advice and consent of the lords spiritual and temporal, and commons, in this present parliament assembled, and by the authority of the same, as follows:

Cases in which contingent remainders capable of taking effect.

"**1.** Every contingent remainder created by any instrument executed after the passing of this act, or by any will or codicil revived or republished by any will or codicil executed after that date, in tenements or hereditaments of any tenure, which would have been valid as a springing or shifting use or executory devise or other limitation had it not had a sufficient estate to support it as a contingent remainder, shall, in the event of the particular estate determining before the contingent remainder vests, be capable of taking effect in all respects as if the contingent remainder had originally been created as a springing or shifting use or executory devise or other executory limitation."

This act will apparently work well in the case of contingent remainders to individuals. I have endeavoured to explain its operation in this respect in the last edition of my Principles of the Law of Real Property (*a*). But in the case of gifts to classes its effect is not so clear. Take the case of *Brackenbury* v. *Gibbons* (*b*). In that case R. Todd, by his will in December, 1854, devised lands to his daughter H. Nundy for life, and after her decease, in case she had no child (which event happened), he gave the

(*a*) Pages 271, 282, 316, 319, 383, 12th ed.

(*b*) L. R., 2 Ch. Div. 417.

same to the child or children of his daughter E. Gibbons, who, either before or after her death, should attain twenty-one, or die under that age leaving issue living at his, her or their death, in fee as tenants in common. At the death of H. Nundy two children of E. Gibbons had attained the age of twenty-one years. No child of E. Gibbons had died under twenty-one leaving issue. There were other children of E. Gibbons who attained twenty-one after the death of H. Nundy. Sir C. Hall, V.-C., decided that the two children of E. Gibbons who had attained twenty-one at the death of H. Nundy took each a moiety to the exclusion of the children of E. Gibbons who attained twenty-one after the death of H. Nundy. His Lordship referred to Jarman on Wills (*c*), where the law is thus laid down:—"If lands of which the testator had the legal inheritance be devised to A. for life, with remainder in fee to the children of A. who shall attain the age of twenty-two, the devise in remainder will be good, for as soon as any child attains twenty-two in the lifetime of A., *the whole remainder vests in him*, subject to open and let in such other children as attain twenty-two in A.'s lifetime; and, on the death of A., those children alone take who have attained twenty-two, to the exclusion of others who may afterwards attain that age: and if, at the death of A., no child has attained twenty-two the remainder fails." And his Lordship added, "As to whether this remnant of the feudal law ought to be altered or not by the legislature I say nothing. There were persons who thought that contingent remainders ought to be abolished, and when the first act preserving contingent remainders from failure in certain cases was passed some years ago, a clause was introduced for giving effect to every gift by way of contingent remainder which would have had effect given to it had it been an executory devise, but the law was otherwise settled." One would have thought it desirable that this remnant of the feudal law should be abolished. But on referring to the Act it will be seen that it remains untouched. The Act only applies "in the event of the particular estate determining before the contingent

(*c*) Vol. 1, p. 239, 3rd ed.

remainder vests." But here, as Mr. Jarman says, the contingent remainder does vest during the continuance of the particular estate.

Before the bill on which this Act was founded was brought in, I had printed and circulated a bill for the same purpose, which was as follows —:

"*An Act for the Amendment of the Law with respect to Contingent Remainders.*"

"**1.** This Act may be cited as 'The Contingent Remainders Amendment Act, 1877.' **Short title.**

"**2.** This Act shall commence and come into operation on the 1st of January, 1878, and shall apply only to instruments executed on or after that date, and to wills and codicils revived or republished by any will or codicil executed on or after that date. **Commencement of Act.**

"**3.** A contingent remainder of an estate of freehold shall, if not otherwise invalid, take effect in possession notwithstanding the want of a particular estate of freehold to support it, in the same manner as it would have taken effect if it had been a contingent remainder of an equitable estate supported by an outstanding legal estate in fee simple. And in like manner a contingent remainder of a copyhold or customary estate shall, if not otherwise invalid, take effect in possession notwithstanding the want of a particular copyhold or customary estate of freehold to support it. **Contingent remainders supported.**

"**4.** The legal estate in the meantime and until such taking effect in possession as aforesaid shall, if not otherwise disposed of, result to the settlor and his heirs or customary heirs, as the case may be, as part of his old estate, or, if the contingent remainder be created by a will or codicil, to the heirs or customary heirs of the testator or other stock of descent according to the rules of inheritance. **Legal estate meantime to result to settlor or his heirs.**

"**5.** The rules as to invalidity by reason of remoteness which now govern contingent remainders of equitable estates shall govern contingent remainders of legal estates, both freehold and copyhold or customary." **Rules as to remoteness.**

The effect of this bill, had it been passed into an act, would have been to preserve the estates of the children of E. Gibbons, who attained twenty-one after the death of the tenant for life. Contingent remainders of legal estates would thereby have been assimilated to contingent remainders of equitable estates, supported by an outstanding legal estate in fee simple. And as Mr. Jarman says (*d*), "Contingent remainders (if we can properly so call them, for they are, in fact, executory interests) of trust or equitable estates, are not governed by the same rule as contingent remainders of legal estates. The former do not, like the latter, necessarily vest or fail upon the determination of the previous estate, but await the happening of the contingency on which they are limited, and must therefore fail, if that contingency be too remote." The only children of E. Gibbons who would have been excluded, would have been those, if any, who were not *born* until after the decease of H. Nundy, according to the rules laid down by Mr. Jarman in his second volume (*e*).

Again, the effect of the present Act is that, under a gift of lands to A. for life, with remainder to his eldest son who shall attain twenty-five, the remainder is still valid if A. has a son who attains twenty-five in his lifetime. The effect of my bill would have been that the remainder to the eldest son would have been void for remoteness, in the same manner as the like remainder of a trust estate would be void for that reason. My bill would have rendered the law of real estate in this respect uniform with that of personal estate. The present Act, though remedial as far as it goes, adds one more to the many anomalies existing in our law.

(*d*) 1 Jarman on Wills, 237, 3rd ed.

(*e*) Vol. 2, pp. 146, 147, 3rd ed.

INDEX.

A.

B.

C.

D.

E.

F.

I.

J.

K.

L.

M.

O.

P.

Q.

R.

S.

T.

Spotted something that isn't quite right?

Let us know and we'll fix it for future reprints. And as a thank you for your diligence, we'll send you a free Sothis book of your choice.

publisher@sothis.press

This page intentionally left blank

Made in the USA
Monee, IL
08 November 2026

68001561R00142